THE WHITE EARTH NATION

The White Earth Nation

RATIFICATION OF A NATIVE
DEMOCRATIC CONSTITUTION

Gerald Vizenor AND *Jill Doerfler*
INTRODUCTION BY *David E. Wilkins*

University of Nebraska Press / Lincoln and London

Chapter 4, "The Constitution of
the White Earth Nation: A Vision of
Survivance" by Jill Doerfler, is based
upon a series of newspaper articles
written between August 4, 2010,
and March 4, 2011, for *Anishinaabeg
Today: A Chronicle of the White Earth
Band of Ojibwe*, the official newspaper
of the White Earth Nation.

The royalties earned from the sale
of this book will be contributed
directly to the White Earth Nation
Book Fund to support students
at the Institute of American Indian
Arts in Santa Fe, New Mexico.

Library of Congress
Cataloging-in-Publication Data
Vizenor, Gerald Robert, 1934–
The White Earth nation: ratification
of a native democratic constitution /
Gerald Vizenor and Jill Doerfler;
introduction by David E. Wilkins. p. cm.
Includes bibliographical references.
ISBN 978-0-8032-4079-7 (pbk.: alk. paper)
1. White Earth Band of Chippewa
Indians. 2. Ojibwa Indians—Legal status,
laws, etc. 3. Ojibwa Indians—Politics and
government. 4. Ojibwa Indians—Government relations. I. Doerfler, Jill. II. Title.
E99.C8V59 2012
323.1197'333—dc23
2012023624

Designed and set in
ITC New Baskerville
by Nathan Putens.

In memory of Vine Deloria Jr.

My son, never forget my dying words. This country holds your
father's body. Never sell the bones of your father and your mother.
JOSEPH THE ELDER, chief of the Nez Perce

To starve a child of the spell of the story, of the canter of the
poem, oral or written, is a kind of living burial. It is to immure him
in emptiness.
GEORGE STEINER, *Real Presences*

The book is an institution of memory for consecration and per-
manence, and for that reason should be studied as a key element
in society's cultural patrimony. In itself, patrimony has the ability
to stir a transmissible feeling of affirmation and belonging. It can
reinforce or stimulate a people's awareness of identity in their territory. A library, an archive, or a museum are cultural patrimonies
and all nations regard them as temples of memory.
FERNANDO BÁEZ, *A Universal History of the Destruction of Books*

Contents

1 Sovereignty, Democracy,
   Constitution: An Introduction 1
   David E. Wilkins

2 Constitutional Consent: Native
   Traditions and Parchment Rights 9
   Gerald Vizenor

3 The Constitution of the
   White Earth Nation 63

4 A Citizen's Guide to the White
   Earth Constitution: Highlights
   and Reflections 81
   Jill Doerfler

Bibliography 95

Contributors 99

THE WHITE EARTH NATION

1

David E. Wilkins

Sovereignty, Democracy, Constitution

AN INTRODUCTION

Sovereignty. Democracy. Constitution. These are mere words. But words, and the often variable meaning or meanings assigned to them by human beings, matter. Associate Justice Oliver Wendell Holmes put it succinctly in *Towne v. Eisner* when he said, "A word is not a crystal, transparent and unchanged, it is the skin of a living thought and may vary greatly in color and content according to the circumstances and the time in which it is used."

However, as the "skins of living thoughts," words, especially those with the convoluted history and confused contemporary status of concepts like *sovereignty, democracy,* and *constitution,* are intimately linked to the ideas of national identity, political authority (whether absolute or constrained, papal or secular), international law and diplomacy, and intergovernmental relations. Such concepts, I believe, are more useful when they have a measure of clarity. As Karl Deutsch, a political scientist, once observed, "A word is only a kind of noise unless we sooner or later use it to lead to a procedure that will tell us whether or not a certain event or fact belongs under the word. The meaning of a word is defined by its limits, by knowing what does not belong under it as clearly as what does. Any word that could include everything and anything has no place in science."

Unfortunately, and despite their centrality to politics, political science, law, American Indian studies, and other fields, the concepts of *sovereignty*, *democracy*, and *constitution*, along with the kindred terms *nation* and *state*, suffer from what Walker Connor in his study, *Ethnonationalism: The Quest for Understanding*, called a "terminological disease." This is because each of these concepts is "shrouded in ambiguity" due to imprecise, inconsistent, and sometimes completely erroneous usage. A veritable "linguistic jungle" encircles each of these important concepts.

As one example, let us look at the concept of *sovereignty*, arguably one of the most, if not the most, critical concepts in indigenous studies and the resurgence of indigenous nationalism. Does sovereignty mean absolute power, supreme legal authority, or merely legal competence? Does it mean popular will, is it ecclesiastically derived, and does it include both external and internal dimensions? Similarly, does *indigenous sovereignty* mean self-governance, domestic dependency, economic vitality, cultural knowledge and integrity, organic connections to the land, something else, or all of the above?

A quick glance at the judicial, policy, and intellectual literature finds, at a minimum, the following variants of *indigenous sovereignty*: savage sovereignty, quasi-sovereignty, primeval sovereignty, residual sovereignty, semi-sovereignty, inherent sovereignty, delegated sovereignty, internal and/or external sovereignty, spiritual sovereignty, mature sovereignty, cultural sovereignty, economic sovereignty, rhetorical sovereignty, ancient sovereignty, artistic sovereignty, and even food sovereignty, among others. Such a plethora of terms makes it difficult to gain any clear and sensible understanding of the actual status of indigenous nations; their inherent authority in internal and external powers; or their actual political relations with other Native nations, states, the United States, or international actors.

Despite this terminological anarchy, the terms sovereignty and Native sovereignty and the related concepts of indigenous democracy and Native constitutionalism are particularly vital concepts within and outside indigenous communities, as the recent social, cultural, and political efforts of the White Earth Nation attest. The reasons will be expounded upon below and in the chapters that ensue.

Early Indigenous Political and Kinship History

Human societies, regardless of their location on the planet, have over time arrived at a remarkably diverse and generally useful set of informal and formal institutional arrangements in a constant effort to maintain relatively stable social, environmental, and cultural existences. Indigenous peoples in North America were, of course, no exception, and for untold millennia they used a plethora of effective social, political, and economic arrangements that enabled them to coexist within the sacred landscapes and waterways they depended on for their identity, sustenance, and subsistence.

While European notions of sovereign authority were originally said to be legitimated by the Christian God and were later supported by the Roman Catholic Church, over time political theorists, beginning with Thomas Hobbes, sought and achieved a vitally important separation between the state, God, and the church; in the process, they devised a hypothetical social contract in which fear-driven individuals living lives considered to be "solitary, poor, nasty, brutish, and short" joined forces for the common purpose of safety and security and then crafted authority-led governments that were not beholden to divine revelation. Later, theorists like John Locke, Baron de Montesquieu, and Jean-Jacques Rousseau, each of whom held less churlish views of human nature than Hobbes, still utilized the social contract framework that Hobbes had concocted. Governments, according to these theorists, "were conceived as the conglomeration of free people willingly surrendering their right to arbitrary action to a superior in return for the guarantee of law and order." Indigenous peoples, of course, as Vine Deloria Jr. and Clifford Lytle noted in *American Indians, American Justice* (from which the previous quotation is also taken), "did not fit into this philosophical framework because there was no contractual right by individuals against Indian society."

For Native nations, then, there was no hypothetical social contract. What virtually all Native peoples possessed and lived within was a very real cultural and political system based on responsibility, clans, and kinship. As described by Ella Deloria in *Speaking of Indians*, "all peoples who live communally must first find some way to get along together harmoniously and with a measure of decency and order. . . . and that way, by whatever rules and controls it is achieved, is, for any peoples, the scheme of life that works. The Dakota people of the past found a way: it was through kinship." "One must," said Deloria, "be a good relative." Being a good relative, a good citizen of society, "was practically all the government there was. It was what men lived by."

Kinship was intimately connected to the clan systems found in most Native societies. Clans linked tribal citizens within nations and also, to a broader philosophical-cultural extent, across nations, so that the idea of an absolute autonomous tribal nation wielding supreme and unaffiliated power did not exist. Atsenhaienton, a Kanien-kehaka and a member of the Bear clan, said, "I think that the clan system breaks down nationalism; it's the nationalism that causes conflict. If we all sat in our clans and discussed the issues we would get away from the nationalism that divides us."

Just as there were no absolutely autonomous Native nations, there were virtually no individual Native leaders who exercised untrammeled power over their fellow citizens. As Russell Barsh noted, "in the indigenous North American context, a 'leader' is not a decision-maker, but a coordinator, peacemaker, teacher, example and comedian. He cannot tell others what to do, but he can persuade, cajole, tease, or inspire them into some unanimity of purpose. His influence depends on his ability to minimize differences of opinion, to remain above anger or jealousy, and to win respect and trust by helping his constituents through death, danger in hard times at his own risk and expense."

European and European American Conceptions of Native Sovereignty and Governance

As we have seen, European and indigenous nations had divergent beginnings and different understandings of concepts like authority, power, and freedom. Furthermore, each Native society viewed self-government, self-determination, and self-education in ways that comported with their own origin accounts, lands, philosophies, norms and values, ceremonies, and languages. As a result, each Native nation was a unique socio-cultural-political body that sought self-fulfillment and maturity on every human level, both internally and externally.

The European invasion of North America, beginning in the fifteenth century, triggered an unprecedented period of violent confrontations interspersed with occasional moments of cooperation between indigenous nations and the various European and later European American polities. Much literature has been written describing how Europeans conceptualized Native nations. The colonial heritage produced at least three principles that would undergird federal policy and law vis-à-vis Native peoples. First, land, under the doctrine of discovery, was believed to ultimately belong to the United States, although Native nations were viewed as holding a lesser use and occupancy title. Second, indigenous peoples were generally held to be culturally, technologically, and intellectually inferior to Europeans and European Americans. Third, despite their diminished land title and allegedly inferior status, Native nations were treated as nations with the capacity to negotiate diplomatic accords and to conduct warfare.

The combined influence of these three principles structured the language used by U.S. policymakers in their general descriptions of the political status of Native nations, particularly insofar as the concept of nationhood was employed. Virtually all the colonial and early U.S. treaties negotiated with indigenous nations referred to them as *nations*. The art of treaty-making and the recognition of indigenous national status explicitly and implicitly entailed recognition of the inherent sovereignty of tribal nations as self-governing polities capable of diplomacy and war.

The next two centuries of the relations between indigenous people and the state were marked by profound changes in every aspect of Native life. The devastating demographic collapse of human life, along with the destruction of much of the flora and fauna; the coercive attempts by federal authorities to devalue and destroy indigenous cultural and political identity; and the dramatic loss of nearly 98 percent of all aboriginal lands left Native nations reeling on every level. Notwithstanding those horrendous events, the resilience of Native peoples enabled them to continue.

Today, the surge (however halting) of democratization that has been sporadically erupting in various parts of the world since the end of the Second World War—from Africa, to Eastern Europe, and most recently in the Middle East with the people-led movements in Tunisia and with the fall of the autocrat Hosni Mubarak in Egypt—has also taken hold in Indian Country, as shown by the constitutional developments taking place within the White Earth Nation.

Developments at the international state level always dominate global attention, but it is on the smaller scale, the indigenous scale, where never-ending experiments in self-governance, self-determination, and national development have been occurring for nearly two centuries, that we can learn vital details about the rule of custom and law, the pursuit of freedom and liberty, and the meaning and exercise of sovereignty. In fact, while Native nations have struggled under the oppressive weight of colonial rule for the better part of the past two hundred years, the reality is that they have been at the center of a vortex of events and their struggle has often culminated in the development of formal and informal constitutions to improve self-governance and to spread power in a manner befitting their ancestral lines.

Nearly sixty aboriginal nations adopted constitutions before 1934, when a second and larger wave of constitutional development was ushered in by John Collier and the Indian Reorganization Act (IRA) of 1934. Under the auspices of the IRA, another 130 Native nations developed constitutions to better reflect their collective desires and, of course, the desires of federal officials as well. This massive surge in constitutional writing (and, in some cases, rewriting) produced the greatest number of constitutions ever devised in an equivalent length of time in the history of the world. Despite persistent misconceptions about these constitutions, many of them did, in fact, broadly reflect the goals of the communities at the time.

Like all national communities, indigenous nations expand, mature, and become more diversified. By the late 1960s and continuing into the present, the doctrine, if not the full practice, of Native self-determination had dramatically arisen, replacing the discredited federal termination policy. As a result, a new desire for constitutional modification or for the construction of new constitutions was unleashed in many Native societies, as community members realized the need to craft more appropriate organic political arrangements to better represent the spirit of their nations.

The White Earth Nation, long a part of the confederated arrangement with the other Anishinaabeg polities, has arrived at the realization that they have matured to the point of devising a document to encompass their present-day understanding of political, legal, economic, and cultural autonomy.

This book, then, is the unique and principled story of how and why the people of White Earth engaged the difficult process of establishing a new constitutional arrangement that links directly with their organic values, lands, and traditions. It critically examines the motives, the strategies, the bedeviling issues, and ultimately the choices they made in crafting their new charter of self-governance, an arrangement that fully comports with who the White Earth people were, who they are now, and who they might become.

2

Gerald Vizenor

Constitutional Consent

NATIVE TRADITIONS AND
PARCHMENT RIGHTS

The American Wild West was a cruel, creepy, and venal entangle-ment of conquest, discovery, diseases, outright extortion, sepa-ratism, and genocide of Native American Indians. Most Native cultures resisted the imperious waves of occidental invasions but were decimated by lethal pathogens and then coerced to negotiate national treaties that actually sanctioned the very contradictions of a constitutional democracy, the generation of federal partitions, exclaves, and reservations. These plenary sanctions never were unequivocal inducements, however slight and crude, to participate in the new democratic manner and solemn federal equity of individual property rights and a Native constitutional polity.

Later, the hasty and arbitrary allotment of treaty land was carried out by national surveys and the obscure metes and bounds of a pervasive, gratuitous, and unjust doctrine that favored immigrant homesteaders and independent yeomen landowners. These devious property rations and reductions of communal Native land obstructed traditional Native sovereignty and governance.

Partition, despotism, and decadence, but not the conventions or chancy covenants of a promissory democracy, followed the brutal dominions, territorial crusades, mercenary capture and abuse, military removal, and genocide against the cultural traditions and continental liberty of Native American Indians. Yet the stories of Natives in these centuries of colonial occupation are about Native survivance rather than cultural victimry.

"Democracy stirs in the wake of American armies," declared Jacques Rancière in *Hatred of Democracy*. These beats and spurs of democratic ironies are more extensive in Native recollections of the past than in the current critical context of armies and corporations in the Middle East and Central Asia. The analogies of democratic anticipation in the wake of armies, traders, the fury of missionaries, and capricious federal agents are manifest in Native communities and on reservations.

Rancière pointed out that the "arguments used to back up the military campaigns devoted to the worldwide rise of democracy reveal the paradox concealed by the dominant usage of the word today." Democracy, he observed, "would appear to have two adversaries. On the one hand, it is opposed to a clearly identified enemy—arbitrary government, government without limits—which, depending on the moment, is referred to either as tyranny, dictatorship, or totalitarianism. But this self-evident opposition conceals another, more intimate, one. A good democratic government is one capable of controlling the evil quite simply called democratic life."

A good Native government of natural reason and survivance must control the "reign of excess," and must certainly do so in the political turns and tease of a constitutional democracy. Rancière stressed that "good democracy must be that form of government and social life capable of controlling the double excess of collective activity and individual withdrawal inherent in democratic life."

The misuse of Native land and the capitalization of resources, minerals, water, and natural stands of timber, was a corporate strategy, not the tender mercies of yeomen landowners. The nature of birds and animals was elusive, and Native totemic visions and associations were shied by the greedy commerce of democracy. Still, in spite of the ironic scenes of democratic encounters, duplicity, and betrayal, the tribute of natural reason and totemic associations, cultural sovereignty, sentiments of survivance, and reminiscence of continental liberty are appreciated in Native narratives.

Native liberty, natural reason, and survivance are concepts that originate in narratives, not in the mandates of monarchies, papacies, severe traditions, or federal policies. Native liberty and survivance are implicit in the savvy ridicule and ironic stories about nationalists, emissaries, and autocrats. Nonetheless democracy is about property, security, and governance, and not always about discrete liberty.

The conventions of survivance create a sense of Native presence over nihility and victimry. Survivance is an active presence: it is not absence, deracination, or ethnographic oblivion, and survivance is the continuance of narratives, not a mere reaction, however pertinent. Survivance stories are renunciations of dominance, the unbearable sentiments of tragedy, and the legacy of victimry.

The dynamic concepts of political and cultural liberty are not only conceived in monotheistic scripture, but in the creative, sacred, dicey, and tricky narratives of Native survivance. Memorable Native narratives are clever and strategic. No traditions, no cultural or political practices dominate the creative chronicles of Native resistance, survivance, and liberty.

"Narrative is always strategic, both for teller and listener, in ways that can range from the callously selfish to the generously prosocial," observed Brian Boyd in *On the Origin of Stories*. "The events that narrative reports may be directly related to present or future choices of action, to situations or people that listeners may become involved with. Or they may offer ways of reasoning about action: analogues or 'parables' to guide our social planning; models to emulate or spurn; or merely images of the range of human character, situations, and behavior, and, in ancestral environments, perhaps also of the behavior of predators and prey."

The Native narratives of cultural traditions, totemic associations, resistance, survivance, and versions of governance were strategic for the deliberation of the sworn delegates and for the principal writer of the Constitution of the White Earth Nation.

"Universal suffrage is not at all a natural consequence of democracy," declared Rancière. "Democracy has no natural consequences precisely because it is the division of 'nature,' the breaking of the link between natural properties and forms of government."

The consent to traditional Native governance was the "natural consequence" of totemic associations, public presentations of concepts and visions, and the common practices of communal reciprocity. The memories of trade routes and stories of natural landscapes, for instance, were direct ancestral connections to cultural situations and to individual positions. Natives, by their traditional practices of cultural sovereignty, survivance, reciprocity, and communal governance, surely envisioned the essence, ethos, and civic character of democracy and liberty.

"Under the traditional forms of government in the United States, it is almost impossible for anyone to play an active responsible part in government unless he is a regularly elected or appointed official," observed Felix Cohen in *On the Drafting of Tribal Constitutions*, edited by David Wilkins. "The practice of many Indian tribes in the past was very different. Any member of the tribe was free to come before the council of chiefs or headmen to put forward some plan that he considered to be for the benefit of the tribe. If the members of the council thought the plan worth trying, they would generally authorize the one who suggested it to organize a group, either of members of the council or of the people, in order to carry out the proposed enterprise."

Democratic Ironies

Native students once recited with unintended irony the patriotic pledge of national allegiance in federal boarding schools, "one nation indivisible," and more than fifty thousand Native soldiers served with military honor in two world wars long before the actual exercise and experience of a constitutional democracy. The federal charters and corporate constitutions, that nasty legacy of military and federal agency dominance, should be revised by legal action, political petitions, and literary irony, and recast at Native conventions and in modern Native constitutions.

The Constitution of the Minnesota Chippewa Tribe is a dubious union of six treaty reservations ordered and structured by federal law and policy on June 20, 1936, and amended on March 3, 1964. The first constitutional article provided that the "purpose and function of this organization shall be to conserve and develop tribal resources and to promote the conservation and development of individual Indian trust property." The mandate of this federal corporate constitution was the direct consequence of the Indian Reorganization Act of 1934, a significant legal reversal of previous federal policies, restrictions, decisions, and dominance. Some thirty years later the actual recognition of inherent Native rights and sovereignty was reviewed in various contexts and confirmed by federal courts.

The Indian Reorganization Act provided for the conservation and expansion of treaty land, and set forth many other provisions and contingencies, including the "right to form businesses and other organizations." The secretary of the interior, however, obviously more powerful than any corporate constitution, "is directed to make rules and regulations for the operation and management of Indian forestry units on the principle of sustained-yield management, to restrict the number of livestock grazed on Indian range units to the estimated carrying capacity of such ranges, and to promulgate such other rules and regulations as may be necessary to protect the range from deterioration," according to the Indian Reorganization Act.

Francis Paul Prucha noted in *American Indian Treaties: The History of a Political Anomaly* that John Collier, the commissioner of Indian Affairs, "aggressively promoted a new policy in Indian affairs that revived tribalism and Indian cultures." The Wheeler-Howard or Indian Reorganization Act of 1934 "adopted much of his program, for the law authorized the renewal or strengthening of Indian tribal governments (with formal constitutions and bylaws) and provided, as well, for tribal corporate economic organizations." There was Native resistance, of course, but in the end "the law created a new structure of tribal councils and elected officials. Although the new forms were not without their faults and traditionalists among some of the tribes would come to ridicule these tribal governments as puppets of the Bureau of Indian Affairs." In fact, the traditionalists were not the only critics of the corporate constitutions and of the council toadies of the Bureau of Indian Affairs and the secretary of the interior.

Native American "sovereignty has been recognized by several European nations," David Wilkins pointed out in *American Indian Sovereignty and the U.S. Supreme Court.* The French and British celebrated the loyalty of Natives in the fur trade and in the colonial and territorial wars. The United States, however, recognized a more substantive domestic version of Native sovereignty in hundreds of ratified treaties, and various states "were forced to concede" a lack of jurisdiction over treaty land and reservations. "Therefore, the legal status of tribal nations derives from their recognized cultural and political citizenship in a tribal nation." This, Wilkins noted, "is wholly unlike the status of other minority groups" in the United States. Commerce, for instance, with foreign nations, states, and "Indian Tribes" is clearly regulated by the Constitution of the United States.

"Between 1778, when the first treaty was signed with the Delawares," reported Prucha, "and 1868, when the final one was completed with the Nez Perces, there were 367 ratified Indian treaties and 6 more whose status is questionable. In addition, a considerable number of treaties that were signed by the Indian chiefs and the federal commissioners were never ratified by the Senate and the president." Moreover, "Indian treaties, when all is said and done, were a political anomaly." The treaties "exhibited irregular, incongruous, or even contradictory elements and did not follow the general rule of international treaties." Indian treaties were "formal agreements," and "had certain characteristics or elements that, although appearing paradoxical or even incomprehensible, did not cancel each other out but existed together in an anomalous whole." The treaties are forever contingent on the plenary powers of the U.S. Congress.

"The cardinal distinguishing features of tribal nations are their reserved and inherent sovereign rights based on their separate, if unequal, political states," observed Wilkins in *American Indian Sovereignty and the U.S. Supreme Court.* These "reserved and inherent sovereign rights" have been "affirmed in hundreds of treaties and agreements" and sanctioned in federal courts.

The Constitution of the White Earth Nation was inspired by native reason, narratives of survivance and cultural traditions, totemic associations, cosmopolitan encounters, and modern democratic constitutions, and was ratified by Native delegates with a determined sense of Native presence, of resistance and survivance over absence and victimry. Many established democracies were inspired by traditions; by revolution, resistance, and war; and by the sentiments of liberty. Some democracies were weakened by consumerism, corruption, political factions, and cynical mistrust of party representation and majority dominance. Native traditions, rights, and liberty, however, have never been an ordinary practice or a structural outcome of democracy. Native constitutional democracies, but not the federal corporate constitutions, are a natural consequence of traditional, communal, and intuitive associations.

Traditional Native governance was based on natural reason, totemic associations, communal reciprocity, theocratic practices, and cultural sovereignty. The individual duties in Native communities were explicit, tacit, and unwritten, and existed in memory and in the sentiments and stories of survivance. Governance by traditions, tribute, and remembrance, however, is not a secure way to safeguard individual rights, equity, and liberty. Cultural reciprocity is a persuasive practice of governance, but memory is not the same as constitutional and legal precedent. Most of the early written constitutions of Native governance were corporate executive councils. The boilerplate constitutions were provided by the federal government. These constitutions were not based on Native experiences or even on the narrative traces of traditional governance.

The Constitution of the White Earth Nation is neither similar to nor commensurate with the federal executive structures of governance. The Constitution clearly merges certain traditional Native principles of governance, for instance community councils and cultural reciprocity, with the necessary political divisions of power—executive, legislative, and judiciary—to provide a narrative structure, process, and rule of law that will ensure the rights and equity of Native citizens in the modern world.

Christian Fritz pointed out in *American Sovereigns* that a "written constitution giving voice to a collective people speaking as the sovereign and directing government was different in theory and practice from previous constitutions. American constitutions were written enactments. The British constitution was a product of tradition and history; it was not enacted, but simply existed. The written American constitutions were the explicit and unilateral orders of the new American sovereign—the people."

Fritz noted the "principle that the people were the sovereign changed the relationship of the governed to their governors. Because the people were the new sovereign, representatives and other governmental officers who served them were subordinate to the new masters, the people. . . . The new American sovereign was not another monarch, but the people operating under written constitutions they created." Moreover, if the "sovereign people created constitutions that established governments, then those governments were necessarily subordinate to their creator, the people. For those who accepted that relationship between the people and their government, the people naturally played a role as the ruler to monitor government." The point of "American constitutionalism is that in America the people are the sovereign who rule through the means of written constitutions." Also, the "essence of the rule of law is that binding law exists above the governors and the governed alike."

Sheldon Wolin pointed out in *The Presence of the Past: Essays on the State of the Constitution* that a "constitution is simultaneously a political and a hermeneutical event." The Constitution of the United States, as a political event, "represented a settlement about power on terms that the leaders of the dominant interests—'interests' defined here simply as amalgams of economic, class, sectional, and ideological elements—agreed upon and believed they could persuade the politically significant part of the population to accept. As a hermeneutical event it was a document whose content was agreed upon by the Founders, although," Wolin argued, "meaning was not. The Founders did not produce *a* particular meaning that was subsequently ratified. Rather, they set in motion a form of politics."

The Constitution of the White Earth Nation was conceived and ratified as a resistance to a federal executive constitution and as a necessary structure and manifestation of Native politics on the White Earth Reservation. The Constitution, moreover, is a hermeneutical event, or an interpretation of traditional communal practices, totemic associations, and the equity of Native reciprocity. The political and hermeneutical events of the new constitution were significant and persuasive and were ratified by the Native delegates who participated over two years in four Constitutional Conventions.

Commercial Constitutions

Charles Beard was the first academic historian to promote a contentious economic theory that described the actual formation, ratification, and practicable structures of the Constitution of the United States. He considered the monetary concerns and the private securities and motivations of the Founding Fathers.

Beard declared in *An Economic Interpretation of the Constitution of the United States*, first published in 1913, that the interests of *personalty*, the securities or personal property of merchants, bankers, and established speculators as compared to the interests of planters and debtors, were advanced as favorable monetary provisions and property concessions in the preliminary versions and ratification of the Constitution. A charge of conspiracy is clearly not the outcome of his serious analysis of the economic interests of the constitutional framers and ratifiers, and yet the very notion of a monetary interpretation of the Constitution has been critiqued by several generations of historians.

The Constitution of the United States was "originated and carried though principally by four groups of personalty interests which had been adversely affected under the Articles of Confederation: money, public securities, manufacturers, and trade and shipping," observed Beard. "The members of the Philadelphia Convention which drafted the Constitution were, with a few exceptions, immediately, directly, and personally interested in, and derived economic advantages from, the establishment of the new system" of the national government.

More than thirty of the actual fifty-five delegates to the Convention in Philadelphia were lawyers or had legal experience.

Thirteen delegates were merchants, six were land speculators, eleven had interests in securities, twelve were plantation slavers, two were farmers, two were scientists, three were physicians, one was a college president, and the others were retired or active in public office. John Jay and Alexander Hamilton were against slavery and supported the African Free School in New York City.

Robert McGuire pointed out in *To Form a More Perfect Union* that the "Constitution of the United States replaced the Articles of Confederation as the law of the land when on June 21, 1788, New Hampshire became the ninth state to ratify the Constitution." The new national government had the "power to tax, along with the authority to settle past federal debts." The government under the Articles of Confederation "had little or no power to raise revenues and had difficulty repaying its domestic and foreign debt."

This general discussion of the political and economic interests of the framers and the constitutional powers of the first national governments is necessary to understand the historical legacies, consequences, and significance of federal constitutions established on treaty reservations in the twentieth century, compared to the recent ratification of the Constitution of the White Earth Nation.

The Articles of Confederation, or the first constitution, inspired by resistance and a sense of collective sovereignty, provided for a union of thirteen state governments to secure the common liberties of sovereign citizens.

The Constitution of the United States established a federal government of states, and the sentiments of citizen sovereignty were restructured by electoral representation and the central rule of law, or by the supremacy of the national government. The notion of citizen sovereignty was converted to the notion of the federal government as the source of power and authority.

Article I of the Constitution provided that the legislative powers of the government "shall be vested in a Congress of the United

States." That sovereign grant of legislative power was not the same as the collective sovereignty of the citizens of the thirteen original states. The same article grants to Congress the power to collect tax and revenue, impose duties and excises, pay debts, borrow money, and "regulate Commerce with foreign Nations, and among the several States, and with Indian Tribes."

The Articles of Confederation provided no such grants or prescribed powers of the government. Merchants, bankers, and investment speculators would directly benefit from these new powers of the federal national government.

McGuire noted that this "change of political institutions was to have a profound influence on the history of the United States," and concluded that there "*is* a valid economic interpretation of the Constitution." However, he continued, "this does not mean that the framers or the ratifiers were motivated by a greedy desire . . . or by some dialectic concept of class or social interest. Nor does it mean that some conspiracy among the founders or some fatalistic concept of 'economic determinism' explains the Constitution."

Charles Beard made similar observations some ninety years earlier in his research on the economic interests of the framers. He argued that the "Constitution was essentially an economic document based upon the concept that the fundamental private rights of property are anterior to government and morally beyond the reach of popular majorities." Moreover, he concluded, the "Constitution was not created by 'the whole people' as the jurists have said; neither was it created by 'the states' as Southern nullifiers long contended; but it was the work of a consolidated group whose interests knew no state boundaries and were truly national in their scope."

Beard pointed out that *The Federalist* "presents the political science of the new system as conceived by three of the profoundest thinkers of the period," Alexander Hamilton, James Madison, and John Jay. Hamilton was an economist, political philosopher, and the first U.S. secretary of the treasury; Madison was a lawyer, philosopher, and the fourth president of the United States; Jay was a revolutionary diplomat and the first chief justice of the Supreme Court. These three inspired political leaders were not planters or debtors, but they were astutely dedicated to the establishment of a national constitutional government. Madison, from Virginia, and Hamilton, from New York, were delegates to the Convention in Philadelphia.

The Federalist introduces an "economic interpretation of the Constitution by the men best fitted, through the intimate knowledge of the ideas of the framers, to expound the political science of the new government." Beard noted that this "argumentation by Hamilton, Madison, and Jay is in fact the finest study in the economic interpretation of politics which exists in any language; and whoever would understand the Constitution as an economic document need hardly go beyond it."

James Madison, the august political philosopher and principal author of the Constitution of the United States, observed in *The Federalist X* that the "diversity in the faculties of men from which the rights of property originate, is no less an insuperable obstacle to uniformity of interests. The protection of these faculties is the first object of Government." Madison, more than any other constitutional framer at the time, anticipated the political passion, dissention, and animosity over the "unequal distribution of property." The protection of "unequal faculties" and the sentiments in the acquisition of property "ensues a division of the society" into various interests. "Those who hold, and those who are without property, have ever formed distinct interests in society. Those who are creditors, and those who are debtors, fall under a like discrimination. A landed interest, a manufacturing interest, a mercantile interest, a monied interest, with many lesser interests, grow up of necessity in civilized nations, and divide them into different classes, actuated by different sentiments and views." Madison prudently declared that the "regulation of these various and interfering interests forms the principal task of modern Legislation, and involves the spirit of party and faction in the necessary and ordinary operations of Government."

Wolin declared in *The Presence of the Past* that over "the two centuries since ratification, the influence of *The Federalist* has, if anything, increased. Its conception of politics and national power has become so ingrained in the American political consciousness that few realize the extent to which they have absorbed a particular theory of the Constitution.

"A theory is not, however, a constitution. Practices consist, first, in offices that designate location of authority, and, secondly, procedures or formalities that legitimate the exercise of power."

Continental Liberty

Chief Joseph and the Nez Perce surrendered with dignity to General Nelson Miles on October 5, 1877, in the Bear Paw Mountains, Montana Territory. The august Native leader was designated the Red Napoleon by General William Tecumseh Sherman, a brutish and sardonic nickname. Likewise the arrogant general deserved to be named the Hoary Napoleon. That military sobriquet, however, did not alleviate in any way the communal desolation and misery of some four hundred anguished survivors of an honorable resistance to the capricious removal, racial separatism, and premeditated injustices inflicted by a constitutional democracy.

The Nez Perce had renounced war and negotiated a surrender. Despite the obvious dishonor of military tyranny and despite faraway moral entreaties, they were detained and transported as prisoners of war to Fort Leavenworth, Kansas. General Sherman was a haughty patriot of ethnic vengeance.

The Nez Perce and millions of other Natives were removed from their ancestral homelands and denied the ordinary principles and petitions of habeas corpus in the continuance of common law and the Constitution of the United States of America. The concept of habeas corpus, though not the formal document, was a similar remedy first practiced in Native traditional cultures.

The civil procedure of habeas corpus protects human rights and secures the liberty of individuals. Natives, however, were considered stateless and were not provided with the ordinary surety of habeas corpus or endowed with constitutional protection from despotism, arbitrary incarceration, cruel and unusual separatism, or a revised depiction of extraordinary reservation rendition.

Chief Joseph, an emissary of peace, visited the U.S. Congress two years later to petition for cultural recognition and to ensure the return of the exiled Nez Perce to their native homeland in the Wallowa Valley of Oregon. Members of the Congress, the cabinet, diplomats, and religious and commercial leaders listened to a memorable, heartfelt entreaty for liberty.

"If the white man wants to live in peace with the Indian he can live in peace. There need be no trouble. Treat all men alike. Give them all the same law. Give them all the same chance to live and grow," Chief Joseph told the audience through a translator. "When I think of our condition my heart is heavy. I see men of my race treated as outlaws and driven from country to country or shot down like animals. I know that my race must change. We cannot hold our own with the white men as we are. We only ask an even chance to live as other men live. We ask to be recognized as men. We ask that the same law shall work on all men." Chief Joseph's speech was translated and published in the *North American Review* in 1879.

The U.S. Congress received fourteen petitions of support for the humane cause of Chief Joseph and the exiled Nez Perce. Otis Halfmoon noted in the *Encyclopedia of North American Indians* that six years later, on "May 22, 1885, the Nez Perce boarded railroad cars in Arkansas City to return home to the reservation.

The charisma and diplomacy of Chief Joseph had prevailed."
The Nez Perce survivors were not permitted, however, to return
to their homeland in the Wallowa Valley. They were removed
to the Colville Reservation in Washington.

Chief Joseph was an honorable emissary of survivance. He
conveyed a sense of presence, resistance, and moral courage
that renounced absence and victimry, and his direct, profound
entreaty has inspired Natives and others for more than a century. He could not have known at the time that his forthright
comments, his ethos and remembrance, the very principles
of democratic governance, justice and representation, would
encourage Natives to create new constitutions on reservations.

Chief Joseph was a philosopher of natural reason, a storier of
the ethical sentiments of continental liberty. His manner and
pronouncements were shared as universal ideas and values, as
the very same principles that have inspired the philosophers and
legislators of democratic governance around the world. *Treat all
men alike. Give them all the same law. Give them all the same chance
to live and grow.* These are the ordinary, steady, and heartfelt
expressions of human rights and native liberty.

Chief Joseph never promoted or petitioned for separatism
by Native traditions or cultural practices. His evident concepts
and associations of human and animal rights were native and
universal; they were not monotheistic, discrete, expedient, or
compromised by political favors. It seems that his native sense
of justice was secured by conscience, experience, and Native
traditions. Despite decades of injustices, he never wavered or
abandoned his dedication to the Native sentiments of survivance and the principles of liberty.

Factions and Liberty

"Complaints are every where heard from our most considerate
and virtuous citizens, equally the friends of public and private
faith, and of public and personal liberty; that our governments

are too unstable; that the public good is disregarded in the conflicts of rival parties; and that measures are too often decided, not according to the rules of justice, and the rights of the minor party; but by the superior force of an interested and over-bearing majority," observed James Madison in *The Federalist X.*

Madison pointed out that a "factious spirit has tainted our public administration." There are "two methods of removing the causes of faction: the one by destroying the liberty which is essential to its existence; the other, by giving to every citizen the same opinions, the same passions, and the same interests."

Chief Joseph and millions of Natives would directly realize the outcome of a century of factions, avarice, political corruption, and the destruction of liberty. Formal and emotive entreaties of reason and justice were either scorned or disregarded, no matter what the manner of political and ecumenical commiserations of the elected members of government.

Many presidents issued peace medals, the ironic emblems of that factious spirit of democratic governance. These medals have become the allegories of political partition and cultural separatism. Politicians and the military rarely honored the concept of peace or the presidential symbols of peace. The dubious merit of the medals lasted only for the elected term of the president. Today, these medals are political anomalies and curiosities in museum collections.

"It could never be more truly said than of the first remedy, that it is worse than the disease," declared Madison. "Liberty is to faction, what air is to fire, an aliment without which it instantly expires. But it could not be a less folly to abolish liberty, which is essential to political life, because it nourishes faction, than it would be to wish the annihilation of air, which is essential to animal life, because it imparts to fire its destructive agency."

Native American Indians encountered the daily corruption of federal agents, missionaries, political factions, and the vengeance of the military. Natives were rarely accorded the rights and mobility of ordinary citizens, and were seldom invited to the political discourse on the enriched and speculative factions and "fire" of constitutional governance, the rule of law, and liberty.

Native Presence

Natives have been considered an absence in history, the silence of translation, separation, and simulations. The estimated populations of Natives, for instance, were consistently understated for obvious political and cultural reasons, and it was claimed that the colonial conquest and occupation of the continent displaced only a million Natives. The government, farmers, ranchers, and land speculators were largely indifferent to the extensive Native knowledge of the environment. Sacred sites, centers of remembrance, and familiar Native places were renamed by the conquerors and stories of sacred and familiar Native places were suppressed, a practice explicitly intended to render Natives a continental absence in history. Consequently, the academic enterprises of ethnography, cultural anthropology, and archeology easily reigned with facile descriptions, comparative commentaries, statistical and cultural models, and other marvelous simulations of Native polity.

Dynamic Native cultures, the crucial economic experiences of continental trade routes, the diplomatic *savoir vivre* of the fur trade, and the mastery of trickster stories and other creative narratives that anticipated postmodern literary discourse were reduced to serve the reductive comparative cultural practices of presumptive science and anthropology.

There were notable scholarly exceptions, of course, such as the symbolic interpretations of culture by Clifford Geertz and the enlightened studies of Native legal systems by E. Adamson Hoebel, but the mundane drivel of untold numbers of scientific studies, structuralist models, dubious empirical documents, federal reports, political- and foundation-favored research, and thousands of doctoral dissertations dominated the interpretations and considerations of Native cultures. This putative archive has engendered simulations, perverted Native epistemologies, and generated a historical absence of Natives.

The dominion of monotheism and the outright denial of human rights and communal practices and, at the same time, the dreary methodological reductions of creative and visionary Native stories contributed to an increase of simulations and the crude romance of Native victimry. Discernible and widespread institutional and commercial simulations of bygone Native cultures, and popular sentiments of Native absence and victimry, dominated contemporary pedagogy and publications in literature, history, and popular culture. The routine simulations of Native absence and victimry inadvertently encouraged ethnic and racial revisionism, savagism, and civilization in motion pictures, in photographic depictions of romantic stoicism, in manifest concoctions of tribal identity and authenticity, and in the translations and reductive stories of absolute and terminal cultural traditions.

The subsequent structural models of traditional Native governance were customarily presented in elaborate circular or orbital hierarchic schemes with figurative connections to the four directions. Some of these structuralist schemes of traditional governance might have been presented in six or seven directions by the incorporation of a Native visionary presence and the Native sentiments of natural reason and totemic associations.

These hierarchic schemes of governance are based on uncertain, if not imagined, traditions and seldom provide for the protection of human rights or the separation of powers into the legislative, the executive, and the judicial. Popes and potentates are anomalies in modern practices of democratic governance, yet the romance of Native theocratic and hierarchic conventions has been promoted as traditional Native governance. Theocracy, however, is a tradition barrier of democracy and liberty. Moreover the current prescriptive orbital models of hierarchy and supremacy, comprised of various echelons of councils and interrelated with the four earthly directions, have become Native parchment barriers that restrain the necessary political divisions of governance, democratic equality, discrete rights, and ordinary passions of liberty.

Certain reservation constitutions were corporate executive models of governance provided by the federal government after the adoption of the Indian Reorganization Act of 1934. The absence of a judiciary and no explicit provisions for the separation of powers in these federal constitutions contributed to factions and to unreserved executive authority. Native constitutions with a discrete judiciary would more likely safeguard sovereignty and natural reason, or Native common law, by the rule of law and the precedent of human rights and liberty.

The Indian Reorganization Act "constitutions and those modeled after them . . . share certain structural weaknesses," observed Eric Lemont in *American Indian Constitutional Reform.* "Most centralize power in a small tribal council, lack provisions for separating power among branches of government, and do not provide for independent courts. In many cases, this centralization of political authority conflicts with tribal traditions or decentralized, consensus-oriented methods for allocating political responsibilities and engaging in collective decision-making."

The traditional schemes of constitutional governance are mainly dependent on translations, customary interpretations, revised narratives, and conceptual traditionalism. Some traditional strategies of governance were inspired by adversity, tragedy, and millennial visions such as the Ghost Dance religion. These schemes of Native moral truth required that the enumerated traditions be established as truisms, an absolute scriptural barrier of rights and customs considered in a democratic constitution. The irony was unintended in the traditional schemes.

Traditions and Barriers

There are at least three narrative models or considerations of traditional Native rights in a new Native constitution. The first is the revisionist or traditional barrier, a circular course of cultural reserves, dictates, and principles of governance. The second narrative is a *copper* barrier, a figurative model derived from the inspiration of an early copper paten or chronicle of totemic Native families. The third narrative model is the parchment barrier of the Bill of Rights in the Constitution of the United States of America.

James Madison considered the narrative distinctions of mere parchment barriers "in theory, of several classes of power, as they may in their nature be legislative, executive, or judiciary." He pointed out that the "next and most difficult task, is to provide some practical security for each against the invasion of the others. What this security ought to be, is the great problem to be solved." He inquired if it would be "sufficient to mark with precision the boundaries of these departments in the Constitution of the government, and to trust to these parchment barriers against the encroaching spirit of power?"

Madison explained in *The Federalist XLVIII*, for instance, that the "legislative department is every where extending the sphere of its activity, and drawing all power into its impetuous vortex." He concluded that a "mere demarcation on parchment of the constitutional limits of the several departments, is not a sufficient guard against those encroachments which lead to a tyrannical concentration of all the powers of government in the same hands."

Benjamin Bailyn proclaimed in *To Begin the World Anew: The Genius and Ambiguities of the American Founders* that the "parchment barriers," or "a few luminous words on paper, would not keep ambitious men from exercising undue power: freedom can be preserved not by glowing statements but by the balance of real forces."

Benjamin Barber wrote in "Constitutional Rights—Democratic Instrument or Obstacle?" that there is a "simple but powerful relationship between rights and democracy: rights entail the equality of those who claim them; and democracy is the politics of equality." His essay was published in *The Framers and Fundamental Rights*, edited by Robert Licht. "Without democracy, rights are empty words that depend for their realization on the good will of despots," noted Barber. Madison "recognized that rights without supporting political institutions were so many 'parchment barriers' to tyranny; this was one reason for his early opposition to a separate Bill of Rights."

Barber declared that without "citizenship and participation, rights are a charade. Without responsibility, rights cannot be enforced. Without empowerment, rights are decorative fictions. A constitution is, after all, a piece of paper, and 'parchment barriers' are never much use against lead and steel and chains and guns."

Judith Best observed in "Fundamental Rights and the Structure of the Government," an essay included in *The Framers and Fundamental Rights*, that the "rule of law emerging from the form of our government—the democratic federal republic, with its separation of powers—is the ongoing guarantee of our fundamental rights. These fundamental rights are expressed in and secured by a competent and balanced governing process, not by mere 'parchment barriers.' It is possible to make a list of fundamental rights, especially in the form of prohibitions on government, and then to emboss them on parchment. One of the dangers of this kind of enterprise, however, is omission—either through lack of foresight or through failure to recognize the potential breadth and complexity of liberty. Awareness of this problem produces disclaimers like that in the Ninth Amendment: 'The enumeration in the Constitution, of certain rights, shall not be construed to deny or disparage others retained by the people.'

"Yes, liberty must be secured against government; but mere prohibitions on anyone, including the government, will be ineffectual unless there is an agent with the 'means and motives' to enforce the prohibition," declared Best. "Thus our founders put their faith in a governing *process* and not in a set of parchment prohibitions."

The advocates of the sacred and Native traditions, the steadfast utopian fanciers of Native theocracies and federal reservations, the cocky cultural revisionists, and the political ideologues envisioned, it would seem, a configuration of governance similar to the conception of a copper barrier of Native ancestors and traditions, otherwise a council of headmen and their families. The copper barrier is analogous to the parchment barrier.

The actual copper paten was a record of nine generations of symbolic leaders and families who associated with the totemic crane, one of five original and traditional totems of the Anishinaabe. The wisdom of Native ancestors is a crucial mediation, but not a barrier to the sentiments of survivance and liberty. The advocates of a figurative copper barrier of ancestors, might, at the same time, protest a modern constitution that provides for an actual system and process of democratic governance, a necessary separation of powers, and the enumeration process and protection of human rights. The obvious premise is that Native ancestors and traditions must sustain natural reason and the sentiments of survivance, rather than hinder or stonewall the creation of democratic constitutions and Native political systems of governance. The memories and narratives of Native traditions cannot survive as constant barriers to the cultural evolution of survivance, *postindian* cultural conditions, and the necessary generation of democracies.

The origin of the word *indian* is a navigational miscalculation, an unintended maritime invention, but the irony became a political simulation of thousands of distinct Native cultures. The simulation of Natives as *indians* has strengthened the notion of Natives as an absence. Surely, most people are now aware of these simulations in literature, history, motion pictures, and popular culture. So, the word *postindian* reduces the significance of the word *indian* by a simple prefix that indicates "after in time," or after the invention of the *indian* and the simulation of Natives. Readers familiar with the word *postindian* may more easily appreciate the distinctions of *indians* and Natives and the legacy of colonialism.

Preamble to Survivance

The Native dissent and resistance to the proposed constitution was moderate at the first White Earth Constitutional Convention. Later on the opposition became more focused, personal, and intense, and became an attempt to influence the forty Native delegates who had been duly sworn to consider Native traditions, the universal concepts of human rights, and the principles and practices of modern governance on the White Earth Reservation.

The resistance to the new constitution was more equivocal than a composed alternative of governance. The delegates, however, dutifully considered a proposed circular "Flow Chart for the Constitution of the White Earth Ojibwe Nation of Anishinaabeg." The center of the scheme was the Central Council surrounded by an orbit of eight divisions, and eight more outer councils in the wider circle. The orbital chart never reached the distinction of a copper barrier that represented inherited Native traditions and totemic associations of leadership. The orbital scheme of governance was never analogous to the contentious concept of a parchment barrier in the early negotiations regarding the inclusion of a specific bill of rights in the Constitution of the United States.

The crucial critiques of the weakness of rights and traditional governance barriers, the shortcoming and uncertainty of stating only certain rights, copper or parchment, did not constrain the hearty communal discussions, considerations, and serious decisions of the delegates during four weekend Constitutional Conventions at the Shooting Star Casino on the White Earth Reservation.

The preamble to the ratified Constitution of the White Earth Nation demonstrates, for instance, the traditional sentiments and principles of survivance, but not the traditional barriers, and at the same time presents the modern concepts of individual rights and the conventions of democratic governance:

> The Anishinaabeg of the White Earth Nation are the successors of a great tradition of continental liberty, a native constitution of families, totemic associations. The Anishinaabeg create stories of natural reason, of courage, loyalty, humor, spiritual inspiration, survivance, reciprocal altruism, and native cultural sovereignty.

> We the Anishinaabeg of the White Earth Nation in order to secure an inherent and essential sovereignty, to promote traditions of liberty, justice, and peace, and reserve common resources, and to ensure the inalienable rights of native governance for our posterity, do constitute, ordain and establish this Constitution of the White Earth Nation.

Native American Indians were excluded for more than a century from the exemplary sentiments of the first sentence of the Constitution of the United States. "We the People" was an exclusive association that would never form a perfect union or establish justice for Natives and for others on the margins of the surety of liberty.

"We the Anishinaabeg of the White Earth Nation" is a pithy declaration of Native presence and survivance over absence and victimry. The preamble is a heartfelt assertion that the Anishinaabeg of the White Earth Nation have sustained a sense of communal polity. The common and singular form of the traditional cultural name of the people is Anishinaabe. The irony and incongruity of constitutional pronouns are no less exemplary than the very exclusion of Natives would provide the destiny of democratic means and models to create the Constitution of the White Earth Nation.

"We the People" seems to be comprehensive, and "looms as the constitutional subject of the United States," noted Michel Rosenfeld in *The Identity of the Constitutional Subject.* The pronoun phrase "merges together the constitution makers and those subject to the Constitution, as well as the governors and the governed," as does the concept of the "social contract" created by Jean Jacques Rousseau.

"We the People" did not represent the entirety of the constitutional subjects of the country, not Natives, slaves, women, immigrants, or even the privileged property owners, and does not express a sense of "genuine unity." Actually the uneasy phrase "embodies a stark contradiction." Rosenfeld pointed out that "'We the People' cannot be fairly said to include the African American slaves then living in the United States." Woman suffrage was not realized until the passage, in 1920, of the Nineteenth Amendment to the Constitution of the United States: "The right of citizens of the United States to vote are not denied or abridged by the United States or by any state on account of sex." Natives were also excluded from land, rights, and ordinary continental liberty. Partition and separatism were the absolute opposites of the fictitious concept of the constitutional subject.

"Constitutions are often portrayed as social contracts, or as pacts among individuals within a polity. Consistent with this metaphor, constitutions are imagined as contracts among individuals within a state, while treaties are, in fact, contracts among states," observed Rosenfeld. "Thus conceived, a contract stands in contrast to custom and tradition."

Many Natives were separated from ancestral homelands by treaties and then removed to reservations. That federal partition and cultural separation denied the subject identity of a constitutional association or social contract. Separatism ensured the historical absence of Natives and endorsed the notion that social contracts and constitutions "stand in contrast to custom and tradition."

The Anishinaabe have endured with a sense of survivance and have resisted the notions of absence and victimry in a new democratic constitution. These encounters of chance and separatism, however, have not provided absolute immunities to political envy, factions, and the contradictions of unity as constitutional subjects in the world.

Rosenfeld pointed out that the "constitutional subject and its identity may be more fragile than would initially appear. Their trajectory and future potential confront manifold obstacles and complexities and require painstaking and belabored deployment on many distinct fronts. They remain, however, the best hope for the legacy of the Enlightenment to endure. And to live up to that hope, the constitutional subject must seek to reconcile self and other in accordance with the precepts of the pluralist ethos. In short, the constitutional subject can and, at best, will combine what we share in common and what separates us to make room for us to coexist peacefully in our plural ways in an atmosphere of equal dignity and mutual respect."

Copper Barrier

The copper barrier denotes, as an analogy and historical figuration, the serious sentiments and visionary recurrence of Native traditions, the association of the original leaders of the crane totem, and the communal observances of the Anishinaabe. The delegates were convinced that it was necessary to consider the significance of communal traditions, the union of stories, the remembrance of the sacred world, Native customs, and reciprocity rather than mere barriers in a *postindian* constitution. The outlook of Native traditions, singular stories of ancestors, and associations of the crane totem convened by inspiration on a copper paten were not, however, directly embraced as signature statements of barriers in discussions of the rights and duties of a modern constitution. The probity and practices of Native traditions were more explicitly conveyed in the actual chapters and articles of recent documents and other democratic constitutions. The reference and figuration of the copper paten as a barrier of Native traditions never restrained the delegates in their enlightened discussions and in the ratification of the Constitution of the White Earth Nation.

The notion of a copper barrier of Native traditions is an analogy to the concept of the parchment barrier in the consideration of a bill of rights in the Constitution of the United States. The copper barrier of Native traditions and the parchment barriers of constitutional human rights are never absolute, and are not always an effective means to protect the Native cultural and individual rights or the expressions of liberty.

Native traditions, for instance, have been translated by various methods, interpreted by diverse scholars, politicians, and literary artists, reconsidered by cultural emendation, and revised and simulated in documents and constitutions. The copper barrier of Native traditions has never been an absolute statute of cultural protection. The narratives of copper barriers are not enactments or sanctuaries of Native traditions, and yet the notions of absolute barriers are misconstrued and easily abused by politicians, commercial interests and governments. The copper barrier is a trace of Native traditions, not a system or process of governance. One of the most conspicuous abuses of Native traditions, for instance, was the near extinction of totemic animals in the fur trade economy.

The parchment barriers and covenants of human rights were uncertain in the early political and philosophical discussions that would include a bill of rights as an amendment to the Constitution of the United States.

James Madison declared in a letter to Thomas Jefferson that he had "always been in favor of a bill of rights; provided that it be so framed as not to imply powers not meant to be included in the enumeration." Madison was concerned, however, that "experience proves the inefficiency of a bill of rights on those occasions when its controul is most needed. Repeated violations of these parchment barriers have been committed by overbearing majorities in every State."

Thomas Jefferson responded that the "Declaration of rights is like all other human blessings alloyed with some inconveniences, and not accomplishing fully it's object. But the good in this instance vastly overweighs the evil." No enumeration of rights and liberties could ever be complete.

The orbital schemes of grand Native councils, headmen, theocracies, and the inherited powers of totemic and spiritual leaders do not provide a convention, barriers, or statutes to protect human rights in Native communities. The inherited and unreserved authority of Native headmen and leaders could easily become the equivalent of an overbearing majority. The circles of spiritual and traditional powers are poetic but not always protective of individual rights in modern and diverse Native communities.

Crane Totem

The Anishinaabe historian William Warren observed in the *History of the Ojibway People* that the families of the crane totem were the first to establish a community at Shaugawaumikong, a sand point near La Pointe on Madeline Island in Lake Superior.

Warren served as an interpreter of French and English at La Pointe, the prominent fur trade post on the island, for about five years starting in 1842. He wrote about Tugwaugaunay, his great uncle, the leader of the great crane families, and about a copper paten or plate with incised figures. The crane was one of the original five traditional totems of the Anishinaabe.

The crane "family hold in their possession a circular plate of virgin copper," observed Warren, "on which is rudely marked indentations and hieroglyphics denoting the number of generations" at Shaugawaumikong and at La Pointe or Mooningwanekaaning. The Anishinaabe name refers in translation to the place of the golden-breasted woodpecker.

Warren examined this curious family register in 1842. There were "eight deep indentations denoting the number" of generations and ancestors of the crane totem at Shaugawaumikong.

Tugwaugaunay was about sixty years old "at the time he showed this plate of copper, which he said had descended to him directly through a long line of ancestors," wrote Warren. "He died two years since, and his death has added the ninth indentation thereon; making, at this period, nine generations since the Ojibways," or Anishinaabeg, "first resided at La Pointe, and six generations since their first intercourse with the whites," or the fur trade and the French.

The Anishinaabe count a generation when the "oldest man in the family has died, and the writer assumes from these, and other facts obtained through observation and inquiry, forty years as the term of an Indian generation."

Warren pointed out that according to "this estimate, it is now three hundred and sixty years since the Ojibways first collected in one grand central town on the Island of La Pointe, and two hundred and forty years" since the first contact with the French. That would mean that the crane families of the Anishinaabe first marked a generation on the copper paten in 1482, ten years before the actual benchmark contact with Natives by Christopher Columbus. The first Anishinaabe contact with others, likely the French, would have been 1602 according to the marks on the copper and the calculations of generations. Warren observed that the "rude figure of a man with a hat on his head, placed opposite one of these indentations, denoted the period when the white man first made his appearance among them. This mark occurred in the third generation" of the crane totem leaders at La Pointe.

Anishinaabe Charter

More than three centuries after the first mark on the copper paten in 1482, the White Earth Reservation was established by federal treaty on March 19, 1867. The reservation is located in three counties, Becker, Clearwater, and Mahnomen, in northwestern Minnesota. The legal boundaries of the removal reservation were established by federal government surveys. The boundary has not changed but the actual Native ownership of reservation land is only a small fraction of the original treaty.

The Constitution of the White Earth Nation was ratified by the sworn delegates on April 4, 2009, more than five centuries after the first totemic representation of the crane families on the copper paten at La Pointe, Madeline Island, Wisconsin.

The reservation was first governed by federal agents, and with the unbidden counsel of Native elders and representatives of the community. Most of the federal agents, who were stony and unlikable, ruled the reservation as an occupied territory held in trust by the federal government. The agents of the uncertain trust were mainly capricious and corrupt in the ordinary administration of the reservation.

The hundreds of original Native families on the reservation had been removed according to the treaty from a wide area of woodland settlements in the northern sections of Minnesota. Alas, federal legislation partitioned the reservation into individual allotments, and subsequent state and federal legislation separated many Native families from each other and from the original treaty land. Natives were separated by federal racialist policies and were removed from the land by legislation that favored the timber speculators of white pine and other natural resources on the White Earth Reservation.

The Progress

Theodore Hudon Beaulieu, the inaugural editor of *The Progress*, clearly articulated the necessity of democratic and constitutional rights in the second issue of the intrepid weekly newspaper published on the White Earth Reservation.

Beaulieu announced in the first issue of the newspaper, March 25, 1886, some twenty years after the federal invention of the treaty reservation, that the "novelty of a newspaper published upon this reservation may cause many to be wary in their support, and this from a fear that it may be revolutionary in character." Moreover, we "shall aim to advocate constantly and without reserve, what in our view, and in the view of the leading minds upon this reservation, is the best for the interests of its residents. And not only for their interests, but those of the tribe wherever they now are residing."

T. J. Sheehan, U.S. Indian agent, arbitrarily declared that the newspaper had been circulated "without first obtaining authority or license so to do from the honorable Secretary of the Interior, the honorable Commissioner of Indian Affairs, or myself as United States Indian Agent."

I observed in *Native Liberty: Natural Reason and Cultural Survivance* that practically "every means of communication by federal agencies about Natives was ironic, and in this instance the mere use of the word 'honorable' was an invitation to mockery. The honorific names of secretaries, commissioners, and federal agents are an eternal summons to ridicule with tricky invectives."

The second issue of *The Progress* was published on October 8, 1887, more than a year after the editor and Augustus Hudon Beaulieu, the publisher, were ordered removed from the reservation, after a favorable federal court decision and a hearing by the subcommittee of the Senate Committee on Indian Affairs.

The editor reported in the second issue that "we began setting the type for the first number of *The Progress* and were almost ready to go to press, when our sanctum was invaded by T. J. Sheehan, the U.S. Indian Agent, accompanied by a posse of the Indian Police. The composing stick was removed from our hands, our property seized." The federal agent charged the editor and publisher "with the voicing of incendiary and revolutionary sentiments at various times." The editor denied the charges and the insinuation that the newspaper violated the federal Indian Trade and Intercourse Act.

The curious indictment was not, of course, based on actual illicit trade with Natives on federal exclaves. The editor and publisher were both Native and citizens of the reservation. The Indian agent may have capriciously surmised that an obscure section of the law could be applied to prevent the publication of a newspaper.

The Act was intended to "regulate trade and intercourse with the Indian Tribes, and to preserve peace on the frontier," and requires that traders obtain licenses to trade with Natives on federal reservations. One section of the law provides that if "any citizen or other person residing within the United States or the territory thereof, shall send any talk, speech, message, or letter to any Indian nation, tribe, chief, or individual, with an intent to produce a contravention or infraction of any treaty or other law of the United States, or to disturb the peace and tranquility of the United States, he shall forfeit and pay the sum of two thousand dollars." The federal government was obviously concerned about Native gossip, ironic revelations, conversations, ecstatic stories of avian flight, and oral strategies of resistance in 1834.

Theodore Beaulieu and many other Natives in the country strongly opposed the passage of the Dawes General Allotment Act of 1887. The feisty editor declared his opposition to the legislation with this headline on the front page of *The Progress*: "Is it an Indian Bureau? About some of the freaks in the employ of the Indian Service whose actions are a disgrace to the nation and a curse to the cause of justice. Putrescent though the spoils system."

The Dawes Act provided for the allotment of communal treaty land to individual Natives, and the "law authorized the president of the United States to proceed with allotments and declare Indians who received allotments to be citizens of the United States." The allotment incentive for citizenship actually favored the corporate exploitation of resources on treaty land. Native people were not fully recognized as citizens of the United States until the passage of the Indian Citizenship Act of 1924.

Sheehan either misinterpreted or deliberately misconstrued the specific provisions of the Trade and Intercourse Act. The Indian agent had never been directly confronted or challenged by a reservation newspaper editor. His response was autocratic, and apparently he was convinced that Natives would have no protections or remedies provided by federal courts or by the United States Constitution.

Beaulieu reported in the second issue of *The Progress* that Judge Nelson of the U.S. District Court "decided that we were entitled to the Jurisdiction we sought. The case came up before him, on jury trial. The Court asserted and defended the right of any member of the tribe to print and publish a newspaper upon his reservation just as he might engage in any other lawful occupation, and without surveillance and restrictions." Beaulieu repeated "the assertion of the silver tongued orator and early patriot Patrick Henry 'if this be treason, MAKE THE MOST OF IT!'"

Theodore Beaulieu clearly demonstrated by his resistance and determination the need for a democratic constitutional government on the White Earth Reservation. The editorial dedication of *The Progress* inspired, in a sense, the sentiments of Native survivance and the ratification more than a century later of the Constitution of the White Earth Nation.

The Progress continued weekly publication on the reservation. The editor and publisher changed the name of the newspaper to *The Tomahawk* in 1903.

Blood Concoctions

The Anishinaabe elders resisted for several generations the unreasonable partitions of cultural, ethnic, and racial policies. The notion of arithmetic blood quantum was concocted as a measure to determine federal services, tribal membership, and identity. The bloody measure was even more punitive because Natives would, through intermarriage, become extinct over time. U.S. statutes, or the permanent laws of the country, name and describe the dicta and regulations relevant to the services provided by the federal government to Natives on treaty reservations, for instance education, health care, housing, land claims, child protection, family justice, and graves protection and repatriation. The severe blood quantum requirements for federal services have been amended, in certain circumstances, to accommodate the specific interests of reservation governments. Many Natives both secular and traditional have declared that family descent, not the racial burden of federal blood quantum, determines cultural identity, personal associations, and citizenship in the White Earth Reservation.

The Minnesota Chippewa Tribe was established by federal legislation as a government on June 20, 1936. Six reservations, White Earth, Leech Lake, Fond du Lac, Bois Forte, Mille Lac, and Grand Portage, were consolidated by a master constitution as a federation with a single government. The purpose of the federation, according to the Revised Constitution of the Minnesota Chippewa Tribe, "shall be to conserve and develop tribal resources and to promote the conservation and development of individual Indian trust property; to promote the general welfare of the members of the Tribe; to preserve and maintain justice for its members and otherwise exercise all powers granted and provided the Indians, and take advantage of the privileges afforded" by the Indian Reorganization Act of June 18, 1934.

The Revised Constitution of the Minnesota Chippewa Tribe was adopted by the assistant secretary of the interior on September 12, 1963, and equivocally ratified by reservation voters on November 23, 1963. The Minnesota Chippewa Tribe provides that membership includes those persons of "Indian blood whose names appear on the annuity roll of April 14, 1941, prepared pursuant to the Treaty with said Indians as enacted by Congress in the Act of January 14, 1889." Anishinaabe children born between April 14, 1941, the date of the annuity roll, and July 3, 1961, the approval date of the "membership ordinance" by federal agents, "to a parent or parents, either or both of whose names appear on the basic membership roll," shall be members according to provisions of an application. Moreover, these contingencies persist today. Children who are "at least one quarter degree Minnesota Chippewa Indian blood born after July 3, 1961, to a member, provided that an application for enrollment" was properly filed, are considered members, according to the Revised Constitution.

The U.S. policies and provisions based on blood quantum as a source of racial evidence have separated families by enumeration and association on reservations. This practice of blood quantum, or crude racial arithmetic, would by procreation and time terminate the people named the Anishinaabe.

The Anishinaabe of the White Earth Reservation convey and demonstrate sanguine notions as citizens and families. "There was no single system for determining who was a part of the community and who was not," observed Jill Doerfler in *Anishinaabeg Today*, the newspaper of the White Earth Nation. "More importantly the Anishinaabe maintained their identity as they adapted to new ways of life at White Earth. Identity was flexible and depended on the choices of individuals. Ultimately, little was agreed upon except that rigid racial designations of 'mixed-blood' and 'full-blood' pushed by the U.S. government investigators were unacceptable and in direct conflict with all Anishinaabeg understandings of identity." The Anishinaabeg "continue to use their own definitions even though they demonstrate a clear awareness" of the ethnic and racial applications of these notions by the federal government.

The Constitution of the Minnesota Chippewa Tribe was conceived, constructed, and advanced by federal bureaucrats with minimal knowledge of Native governance. The Constitution was an expedient federal corporate charter, ostensibly a federation of six reservations. The federal charter established a strong executive with advisory committees, but with no separation of powers or judiciary. There are indeed no real divisions of power in the government. The Tribal Executive Committee, for instance, "shall be authorized to manage, lease, permit, or otherwise deal with tribal lands, interests in lands or other tribal assets; to engage in any business that will further the economic well being of members of the Tribe," and to borrow money from the federal government. The articles of the charter are redundant, unclear, and largely unreadable by ordinary citizens.

The White Earth Reservation is the largest in the federation, and there are specific treaty, charter, and constitutional issues that should be determined by the reserved legislative and judicial powers of the individual reservations, not exclusively decided by the Tribal Executive Committee.

The Tribal Executive Committee decisions about individual reservation resources, for instance, and the actual division and distribution of land claims and other natural resource settlements could be adverse to the citizens of the White Earth Reservation. For the obvious reasons of credible governance and many other cultural, economic, and political objectives, a new constitution was proposed to separate the White Earth Reservation from the jurisdiction of the corporate federation of the Minnesota Chippewa Tribe.

Erma Vizenor, chief of the White Earth Reservation, was reelected for a second four-year term of office in 2008. She had clearly articulated during the election campaign a determination to create a new constitution that would provide a separation of powers into the executive, legislative, and judicial, and to directly protect the rights of citizens. A separation of powers would fairly protect the cultural sovereignty, treaty resources, and land claims of the White Earth Reservation. The ratification and ultimate passage of a referendum on the new constitution would mean the inevitable separation from the reservation federation of the Tribal Executive Committee and the Minnesota Chippewa Tribe.

Convention Delegates

Chief Erma Vizenor invited reservation communities to nominate eligible citizens to serve as official delegates to the White Earth Constitutional Convention. Furthermore, she provided for the nomination of two at large delegates to serve on the Constitutional Convention. Erma Vizenor, who is related by marriage, nominated me as one of two at large delegates, and later in the constitutional proceedings she named me the "principal writer" of the Constitution of the White Earth Nation.

The Constitutional Convention convened for the first time on October 19 and 20, 2007, at the Shooting Star Casino Hotel, White Earth Reservation, Mahnomen, Minnesota. Tribal Judge Anita Fineday presided over the oath, a solemn promise to serve with integrity as delegates to consider a new constitution. That evening and the following day, the delegates met in groups of five to consider the course and significance of discussions about the general content of the proposed Constitution of the White Earth Nation.

The delegates used the words "reservation" and "nation" in almost the same sense at the start of the Convention. Later in the discussions, however, a distinction was clearly made between the treaty reservation, cultural sovereignty, testament of ancestors, and the relevant rights and constitutional declarations of a nation.

The delegates eagerly pronounced their confidence in the inauguration of a new constitution, and, at the same time, many delegates raised serious issues about the definition of a reservation citizen by blood quantum or by family descent. The social or team word "member" was renounced in favor of "citizens" of a nation. The delegates were divided over the issue of federal blood quantum policies and family descent by the end of the second convention. Fewer than half the delegates voted to stay with the arithmetic division of blood quantum to determine the status of citizens. After several hours of intense discussions, the delegates who supported the blood quantum rules became more determined, and several delegates revealed critical racial standpoints about intermarriage. The subject was no longer productive. I was obliged, much later, as the principal writer of the new constitution, to accommodate the two intense positions of federal blood quantum and family descent as the description of the word "citizen" in the ratified Constitution of the White Earth Nation. Some delegates were worried that recognition of family descent would increase the actual number of citizens and therefore reduce the available federal health care and other services on the reservation. These were significant concerns, and the sentiments continue to be controversial.

Chapter 2 of the Constitution, entitled "Citizens of the White Earth Nation," contains two articles about citizens. The first article provides that "Citizens of the White Earth Nation shall be descendants of Anishinaabeg families and related by linear descent to enrolled members of the White Earth Reservation and Nation, according to genealogical documents, treaties and other agreements with the federal government of the Unites States." The second article provides protection for those citizens who support the racial arithmetic of federal blood quantum. "Services and entitlements provided by government agencies to citizens, otherwise designated members of the White Earth Nation, shall be defined according to treaties, trusts, and diplomatic agreements, state and federal laws, rules and regulations, and in policies and procedures established by the government of the White Earth Nation." These two articles of the Constitution were discussed and ratified without opposition, and serve the interests of those who describe a citizen by family descent and those who rely on blood quantum certificates. I wittingly wrote the two articles without using the racialist federal words "blood quantum."

I declared in my introductory comments as a delegate that in the near future the Constitution of the White Earth Nation would be taught in public schools. I was probably more idealistic than some other delegates about the creation of an actual constitutional document. I had my doubts, nonetheless, about how the diverse and ardent views of forty delegates could be represented by promise, justly negotiated, and resolved by group discussions into the language of a congruent constitution. Some delegates and observers espoused notions of racial separatism. The intense convictions of racial and cultural partitions are not easily reconciled with native associations, or with the enlightened instructions of genetics, or with an appreciation of the politics of race. Most of the delegates were determined that there would be no racial exclusions, no cultural separatism, and no compromises of Native ancestors in the creation of a document of individual rights, duties, and principles of governance, justice, and liberty.

Robert Dahl pointed out contrary circumstances in the necessary compromises made by delegates to the Convention of the Constitution of the United States. "The delegates had to confront still another stubborn limit: the need to engage in fundamental compromises in order to secure agreement on any constitution at all. The necessity for compromise and the opportunities this gave for coalitions and logrolling meant that the Constitution could not possibly reflect a coherent, unified theory of government," Dahl observed in *How Democratic Is the*

American Constitution? "Compromises were necessary because, like the country at large, members of the convention held different views on some very basic issues." The White Earth delegates faced similar compromises in the deliberations over sovereignty, rights, representation, traditions, and the definition of a citizen.

The second Constitutional Convention was held on January 4 and 5, 2008. The Shooting Star Casino Hotel was a comfortable and convenient place to schedule the four weekend constitutional conferences. Delegates arrived in the early afternoon and convened for dinner, which was followed by general discussions. The delegates stayed overnight and had a full day of discussions in designated groups. At the end of the day summaries of the eight discussion groups were presented for discussion by the entire Convention.

The third Constitutional Convention was scheduled on October 24 and 25, 2008. The number of delegates in attendance had slightly but steadily decreased with each convention. I demonstrated my concern that the attendance of delegates would be eroded to a bare majority if there were more than four Constitutional Conventions. Erma Vizenor was persuaded by my argument and declared that ratification would be considered on April 3 and 4, 2009, at the last Constitutional Convention.

The forty sworn delegates were recognized citizens of the White Earth Reservation. Erma Vizenor requested nominations of delegates and alternates from ten Native community councils. Seven of the Native community councils are located on the reservation: Pine Point, Rice Lake, Callaway, Naytahwaush, White Earth, Elbow Lake, and Mahnomen. Three other Native community councils are located in Minneapolis; in the Iron Range near Duluth; and in Cass Lake, including White Earth citizens who were living on the nearby Leech Lake Reservation. Two delegates were nominated at large. Three delegates were selected from the community council in Cass Lake. Twenty-six delegates were selected from the seven community councils on the White Earth Reservation. Five were selected from the Iron Range, and four from Minneapolis.

Most of the delegates were elders (more than sixty years of age), and some were retired. No delegates were lawyers. More than half of the delegates had completed college courses through extension education on the reservation, and twelve of the forty delegates had earned one or more academic degrees. Two delegates were college teachers, one delegate was a retired firefighter from Minneapolis, two delegates worked in health services, one delegate directed a youth council, one delegate was a musician, one delegate was a Head Start teacher, one delegate directed human relations at the casino, and seven delegates were employed by various federal agencies on the reservation. One delegate was a former elected member of the tribal council. At least four of the forty delegates were honorably discharged veterans of military service. Only one elected member of the incumbent tribal council participated in the delegate group discussions.

The chief tribal court judge of the White Earth Reservation did not attend any of the Constitutional Conventions. Chief Erma Vizenor, who had earned a doctorate from Harvard University, convened the conventions and participated in the group discussions, but she was not a delegate.

Erma Vizenor named me the principal writer and appointed three advisors to discuss the proposed drafts of the constitution: Jill Doerfler, assistant professor of Indian Studies, University of Minnesota, Duluth; JoAnne Stately, vice president of development for the Indian Land Tenure Foundation; and Anita Fineday, chief Tribal Court judge, White Earth Nation.

The Constitution of the United States became a general guide to the preparation of a prudent and practical representation of governance, but the only specific references were secured, of course, from the Bill of Rights. At first the most difficult problem for me was to find a form, a general structure, and direct descriptive language to document the narratives of rights and duties of

Native governance. I turned to the Constitution of Japan, one of the most recent democratic constitutions in the world, for clarity of content, form, and understandable narrative structure.

The Constitution of Japan provided uncomplicated chapters that described the modern practices of governance. I adapted the chapter style with thematic divisions, such as executive, legislative, judiciary, advisory councils, elections, citizenship, Native rights, and the duties of elected representatives. My adaptation of this forthright and uncomplicated structure made it much easier for me to consider and organize specific chapters on independent governance. I then devised an organization strategy, actually an essential strategy to consider a wide range of Native narratives, sentiments, principles, practical and legal statements, provisions, and protections from many, many sources, including the critical summaries of delegate discussions, treaty rights, the extant federal executive constitution, federal and international laws, and many other sources of modern Native governance, preservation, reciprocity, and security.

The account of my structural strategy must be reduced to a general description because the actual practice was much more complicated, a strategy partly created in the process of writing the constitution. In other words, the narrative of my strategy to write a constitution is an original Native story. I literally cut and separated out relevant statements and documents from many sources and then created categories of governance. I created more than a dozen categories, using literally hundreds of statements and documents, such as councils, Native rights, totemic association, sovereignty, free speech, artistic expression, possession of firearms, and the prohibition of banishment. Finally a fundamental structure and organization emerged, and from the transcription of many sources the chapters of the constitution began to take shape. The duplications were combined or eliminated, and each chapter was rewritten many, many times for brevity and clarity.

I am convinced now that no one else could have written the Constitution of the White Earth Nation that was ratified by the delegates on April 4, 2009. Only an active delegate could have created a narrative of Native governance, and only someone with extensive experience as a creative writer, journalist, and essayist could have organized the necessary summaries of delegate discussions and constitutional documents into pertinent categories to prepare the proposed constitution. I was seventy-four years old and a university professor that spring when the Constitution was ratified, and had published more than thirty books about Native history, literature, and cultural studies. A younger writer and delegate might not have been able to demonstrate the native capacity to gather the experience and intellectual energy, political, practical, and literary, or the train of original philosophical concepts of totemic association, natural reason, and survivance that were critical and necessary. These notions and concepts were precisely articulated in the Constitution of the White Earth Nation.

The Articles of Confederation and the Constitution of the United States were created by a revolution, and pronounced the absolute integrity of that revolution. The Constitution of Japan was created by an extraordinary military order. General of the Army Douglas MacArthur, supreme commander of the Allied Powers in the occupation of Japan, directed his senior command officers to create a draft of a constitution that renounced war, abolished feudalism, and provided suffrage for women and political parties. The document was drafted in about two weeks and became the first and permanent democratic Constitution of Japan.

The Constitution of the White Earth Nation is not a document of revolution, and it is not a document prepared by supreme military officers. The Constitution was created in the spirit of resistance and independent governance, by the sentiments of Native survivance, by the inspiration and vision of the forty delegates in discussions, agreement, opposition, and compromise, and by the dedication and integrity of Chief Erma Vizenor. There is no other constitution in the world that contains the profound sentiments of survivance, natural reason, and the native capacity of continental liberty.

The last review session of the advisory committee convened on January 9, 2009, at the Café Brenda in Minneapolis to discuss the final recommendations, suggestions and minor language changes to the proposed constitution. Jill Doerfler suggested an expansion of the community councils, especially the specific reference to a youth council. I made the necessary changes and prepared the final formal version of the Constitution for consideration and ratification by the delegates.

The delegates received copies of the proposed constitution and were invited to prepare written questions for a general discussion. Each and every article was read out loud, and the delegates discussed the content and purpose of the articles. Necessary changes were made with the full participation of the delegates. The article on the appointment of the chief judge, for instance, was questioned by several delegates and by observers at the Convention. The critical point was that too much political power might be invested in the appointment of chief judge. Earlier, the chief judge had argued in favor of an appointment because unpopular court decisions could influence the election of judicial candidates. That query was fully discussed by the delegates and others, and the article was changed to read that the chief judge would be elected, not appointed. The delegates voted unanimously to approve the revised article.

I created a chance article, an ex officio article about the appointment of an ex officio legislator, without consulting the advisors or any other delegates. The chance article was included in the proposed draft of the constitution distributed to delegates at the last Convention. As the articles were read, discussed, changed, and approved, the ex officio chance article surprised the advisors, delegates, and Erma Vizenor. I boldly reread the chance article, the appointment of an at large legislator to represent the interests of urban community councils, and asked for a formal motion to approve the article. The purpose of the chance article was to initiate and encourage the representation of urban Natives by an ex officio appointment to the Legislative Council. Ten times more Native citizens live in urban areas than on the reservation. The initiation of a wider representation of citizens in the new democratic constitution was necessary.

I asked the delegates for a motion to approve the chance article, and expected the majority delegates from reservation community councils to oppose the chance article. My routine question for a motion that afternoon was first met with avoidance and silence. The delegates were apparently reading the chance article several times. Finally there was a motion to consider, and then, before a second to the motion, or any discussion, an elder delegate presented a motion to amend the chance article. I was certain at the time that the article was about to be revised and twice amended to obscurity, but instead, and much to my surprise, the delegate moved that the article be amended to state that the proposed representative be elected, not appointed ex officio, to the Legislative Council. The approval of the first amendment to the article was also interrupted by a second amendment to increase the number of elected representatives from one to two. The delegates voted unanimously to approve the newly revised article. Chapter 6, article 7, provides that "two citizens of the White Earth Nation shall be elected at large to serve constituencies outside the White Earth Reservation in the State of Minnesota."

The Constitution of the White Earth Nation was duly ratified by sworn delegates on Saturday, April 4, 2009. The ratification was by secret ballot of the twenty-four delegates present. Sixteen delegates voted for ratification, and eight delegates voted against ratification. The Constitution of the White Earth Nation must be presented to eligible citizen voters in a referendum. There are more than twenty thousand citizens of the White Earth Nation.

I properly completed the supplementary changes approved by a majority vote of the delegates, including the addition of two elected members of the Legislative Council from outside the reservation community but with residence in Minnesota. The changes in the final version of the document were only minor. The Constitution of the White Earth Nation was posted on several websites, and the entire new constitutional document, with general explanations and short definitions of special words, such as "survivance," and "continental liberty," was published in *Anishinaabeg Today*, the official newspaper of the White Earth Nation.

The Constitution of the White Earth Nation provides and ensures a continuation of the Native practices of reciprocity, cultural survivance and sovereignty, the advice of community councils, and the foundations of Native reason and common law. The Constitution confirms in conscience and by custom the principles of modern governance, common justice, and native continental liberty. The Constitution of the White Earth Nation entitles the delegates and citizens to say with confidence, "I know my rights."

I conveyed to the delegates at the last Convention that the upstanding discussions over four weekend conferences and my concentration on the traditional principles, duties, and rights of Native citizens discussed at the conventions had produced an extraordinary historical document that would endure any political contests, renunciations, or gainsayers of democratic governance in the future.

I proclaimed in my final presentation to the delegates my heartfelt respect for the communal process of Native sovereignty.

By this Constitution of the White Earth Nation we become a nation that advances the formal practices of governance, cultural sovereignty, liberty, suffrage, justice, and the rights of citizens.

By this Constitution we exercise a new political power and communal duties derived from the traditional practices of the Anishinaabeg. These were the cultural practices of continental liberty, reciprocity, courage, and the survivance of our ancestors. And by the legacy of other constitutions, documents, and the perceptive ideas of liberty inspired by the Magna Carta, we become a new democratic nation.

Magna Carta at White Earth

The Magna Carta was the foundational chronicle of liberty; it was first issued almost eight hundred years ago in England. This ancient, original document considers grievances over feudal land, capricious taxation, and the autocratic justice of the monarchy.

The Magna Carta of 1215 announced, for instance, that no person would be imprisoned or exiled without the lawful judgment of his peers. Later these principles of fundamental justice were provided in the Habeas Corpus Act of 1679 in England.

Mention of the Magna Carta and that legacy of liberty was not altogether appreciated at the last Convention. Several delegates and participants could not understand why a reference to an obscure ancient chronicle was necessary. I tried to explain that the Magna Carta was a legacy of rights and liberty embraced by every liberal and democratic constitution and government in the world. The Magna Carta was a fortuitous influence, along with natural reason and Native traditions, in the presentations and discussions of the delegates at the four Constitutional Conventions.

The Constitution of the United States provides in article 1, section 9, that the "privilege of the Writ of Habeas Corpus shall not be suspended, unless when in Cases of Rebellion or Invasion the public Safety may require it."

The Constitution of the White Earth Nation prohibits exile or banishment, for instance, a sentiment conveyed by many cultures in the world, and this widespread notion preceded the chronicle of the Magna Carta. The sentiments of survivance and liberty are surely a celebration of natural reason that prevailed in Native cultures and in the formal declarations of democratic constitutions.

"Magna Carta did not grant liberty; it granted liberties, lots of them," declared Paul Halliday in *Habeas Corpus: From England to Empire.* Habeas corpus was "fundamentally an instrument of judicial power derived from the king's prerogative, a power more concerned with the wrongs of jailers than with the rights of prisoners. Only fitfully would it become the means by which aspirations external to law, concerned with liberty claims, might be realized." Moreover, habeas corpus "went to new imperial dominions by common law. But colonial subjects in such dominions generally clamored for a habeas corpus act of their own."

The Anishinaabe were not directly swayed by habeas corpus as a common law of colonial dominions, but they practiced natural reason and survivance based on cultural reciprocity and totemic associations to secure hemispheric trade routes and a sense of continental liberty. The sentiments of habeas corpus and liberty were only fitfully realized on the federal partitions of treaty reservations.

Tom Bingham, senior law lord of the United Kingdom, observed in *The Rule of Law* that the Magna Carta "did not embody the principles of jury trial, which was still in its infancy, or habeas corpus." The "Magna Carta was an event that changed the constitutional landscape in this country and, over time, the world."

The Magna Carta declared that no monarch was above the law. This document became one of the most significant influences in the development of common law and subsequent constitutions around the world. The Constitution of the White Earth Nation declares a solemn association of these Native and occidental traditions of human rights and liberty. Elective Native leaders were not above the law: not by inheritance, not by tradition, and not by any custom.

"Magna Carta expressed a deal between church and state, barons and king, city merchants and royalty, wives and husbands, commoners and nobles," declared Peter Linebaugh in *The Magna Carta Manifesto.* The Magna Carta was the "proud product of rebellion," and, in a colloquial comment, the document "puts an emergency brake on accelerating state despotism."

The Second Magna Carta, a marvelous anonymous document, was first published in 1771, sixteen years before the adoption of the Constitution of the United States. Linda Colley noted in *Taking Stock of Taking Liberties,* published in connection with an exhibition at the British Library, that the Second Magna Carta called for "forty-eight representatives from the American Colonies (including some for the 'Indian Nations') to be allotted seats at the Westminster Parliament." The American Revolution concluded that ingenious representation of Native nations at Parliament.

Colley pointed out that "British political arrangements had always proved especially favourable to liberty" and that intervals of "dramatic action involving protest and political change were interspersed over the centuries with periods of relative quiet, complacency, reaction and sometimes repression." The "degree of freedom individuals have been able to enjoy has often been determined by their level of wealth, and by the nature of their religious allegiance, gender and ethnic origins."

Singular Constitution

The Constitution of the United States was proposed and adopted by unanimous consent and signed by thirty-nine delegates at the Constitutional Convention in Philadelphia on September 17, 1787. There were seven articles, including the last article, which states that the "Ratification of the Conventions of nine States, shall be sufficient for the Establishment of this Constitution between the States so ratifying the Same." Delaware was the first state to ratify on December 7, 1787. New Hampshire, the ninth state, confirmed the ratification on June 21, 1788. The Constitution was actually ratified later by all thirteen states. The Constitution of the United States created a government on March 4, 1789. George Washington was elected the first president and took the oath of office on April 30, 1789.

"The fact that we purport to follow and be bound by the Constitution that was proposed in 1787, ratified in 1789, and formally amended just 27 times," wrote Laurence Tribe in *The Invisible Constitution,* "is due, in large part, to the fact that it *is* a single and singular text, one writing, that memorializes the commitments defining us over the course of time in a ways that neither our physical territory nor the multiple ancestral origins of our nation can. Indeed, the physical writing itself—from the parchment signed in Philadelphia in 1787 and still carefully preserved at considerable expense in the National Archives to the numbered copies of the original that circulated physically throughout the several ratifying states—is almost instinctively treated with a devotion ordinarily accorded only to an object of national veneration, rather than any mere statute."

Cultural Sovereignty

The Constitution of the White Earth Nation was conceived by a Native stance of resistance, by the shared sentiments of survivance, by the associations of continental liberty, and by the native intuition of cultural sovereignty and democratic constitutional governance. The declaration and protection of human rights is a universal sentiment and narrative that was embodied in a singular document and ratified by the delegates in the Constitution of the White Earth Nation.

The first ten amendments to the Constitution of the United States, the Bill of Rights, provide the foundations of liberty: that there shall be no law respecting religion or prohibiting free expression thereof, freedom of speech, assembly and petition for redress of grievances, the right to keep and bear arms, no unreasonable searches or seizures, due process of law, speedy and public trial, no excessive bail, and the stipulation that powers not delegated to the United States by the Constitution are reserved to the States respectively, or to the people. The Bill of Rights was ratified in 1791. The Constitution has been amended only twenty-seven times in more than two hundred years.

"The American commitment to freedom of speech and press is the more remarkable because it emerged from legal and political origins that were highly repressive," observed Anthony Lewis in *Freedom for the Thought That We Hate*. "The colonists who crossed the Atlantic in the seventeenth century came from an England where it was extremely dangerous to utter a thought that differed from official truth. The state defined what was allowable in politics and, perhaps even more rigorously, in religion."

The Fifth Amendment, ratified in 1868, at the same time the White Earth Reservation was established by federal treaty, provides that "Representatives shall be apportioned among the several States according to their respective numbers, counting whole numbers of persons in each State, excluding Indians not taxed."

Yes, "Indians not taxed."

The Anishinaabe, by the stories of resistance, courage, political and artistic irony, and by natural reason and a sense of survivance, anticipated this extraordinary moment of continental liberty. The Anishinaabe delegates to the four conventions, taxed or not taxed, considered, compromised, and ratified the Constitution of the White Earth Nation.

The Constitution of the White Earth Nation provides in each chapter a crucial composition of checks and balances, a distinct organization of the powers, measures, limitations, and constraints of three branches of government; the executive, legislative, and judicial. The composition of these powers of governance would embrace the obligatory advice of the community councils: the Council of Elders, the Youth Council, and other future community or association councils provided for by the Constitution.

The Constitution of the White Earth Nation contains two necessary preambles. The first preamble announces the sentiments of cultural sovereignty and continental liberty, and the second preamble is a declaration of essential political sovereignty and inalienable rights. There are twenty chapters and one hundred eighteen specific articles on the branches of the government and the rights of the citizens.

The sworn delegates at the fourth and final Constitutional Convention at the Shooting Star Casino in Mahnomen, Minnesota created by the ratification of a distinct document of Native governance a great and memorable moment in the history of the White Earth Nation and the United States of America. The Constitution of the White Earth Nation ensures the continuation of compassionate reciprocity, cultural sovereignty, and the Native rights of survivance in perpetuity.

Ethos of Governance

Native totemic associations and practices of reciprocity created a sense of survivance, and stories of presence created a communal ethos and narratives of governance and continental liberty. Native governance was never contingent on revolutions or scriptures; not until, of course, Natives were removed to exclaves by a constitutional democracy. Federal policies of separatism were reversed after several generations in an obscure revision of assimilation and agency dominance, and Natives were encouraged to establish modern constitutional governments. These new federal constitutions were corporate charters that favored an executive council but not a judiciary or an elected legislature.

"In past years many Indian tribal councils have tried to operate under written constitutions prepared by the Indian Office," noted Felix Cohen in *On the Drafting of Tribal Constitutions.* "Frequently the Indians and even the officers of the tribe have not been familiar with the provisions of these constitutions, and the constitutions have been merely scraps of paper. This has not been the case where the Indians themselves have determined the forms of their own self-governance."

Many Natives have evaded charter constitutions and executive councils that serve only the commercial interests of communities and treaty reservations. That political resistance to the power of executive councils has inspired many Natives to renounce federal corporate constitutions and create by formal conventions more enlightened democratic systems of Native governance. Erma Vizenor and the forty sworn delegates at four Constitutional Conventions have created by formal deliberation and ratification one of the most significant independent Native constitutions in the country.

"Democracy is neither a form of government that enables oligarchies to rule in the name of the people, nor is it a form of society that governs the power of commodities," declared Jacques Rancière in *Hatred of Democracy.* "Democracy is as bare in its relation to the power of wealth as it is to the power of kinship that today comes to assist and to rival it."

Democracy "is not based on any nature of things nor guaranteed by any institutional form. It is not borne along by any historical necessity and does not bear any. It is only entrusted to the constancy of its specific acts. This can provoke fear, and so hatred, among those who are used to exercising the magisterium of thought. But among those who know how to share with anybody and everybody the equal power of intelligence, it can conversely inspire courage, and hence joy."

3

The Constitution of the White Earth Nation

Preamble

The Anishinaabeg of the White Earth Nation are the successors of a great tradition of continental liberty, a native constitution of families, totemic associations. The Anishinaabeg create stories of natural reason, of courage, loyalty, humor, spiritual inspiration, survivance, reciprocal altruism, and native cultural sovereignty.

We the Anishinaabeg of the White Earth Nation in order to secure an inherent and essential sovereignty, to promote traditions of liberty, justice, and peace, and reserve common resources, and to ensure the inalienable rights of native governance for our posterity, do constitute, ordain, and establish this Constitution of the White Earth Nation.

Chapter 1: Territory and Jurisdiction

The White Earth Nation shall have jurisdiction over citizens, residents, visitors, altruistic relations, and the whole of the land, including transfers, conferrals, and acquisitions of land in futurity, water, wild rice, public and private property, right of way, airspace, minerals, natural resources, parks, and any other environmental estates or territories designated by and located within the boundaries of the White Earth Reservation, as established and described in the Treaty of March 19, 1867, and over the reserved rights within the ceded waterways and territories of the Treaty of 1855.

Chapter 2: Citizens of the White Earth Nation

ARTICLE 1 Citizens of the White Earth Nation shall be descendants of Anishinaabeg families and related by linear descent to enrolled members of the White Earth Reservation and Nation, according to genealogical documents, treaties, and other agreements with the government of the United States.

ARTICLE 2 Services and entitlements provided by government agencies to citizens, otherwise designated members of the White Earth Nation, shall be defined according to treaties, trusts, and diplomatic agreements, state and federal laws, rules and regulations, and in policies and procedures established by the government of the White Earth Nation.

ARTICLE 3 The Anishinaabeg and their descendants shall have the right to appeal to the President and to the White Earth Court any decisions that deny citizenship in the White Earth Nation.

ARTICLE 4 No person or government has the privilege or power to diminish the sovereignty of the White Earth Nation.

Chapter 3: Rights and Duties

ARTICLE 1 The White Earth Nation shall make no laws that would establish a religion, or laws that would deny the free expression of religion, speech, or of the press and electronic communication.

ARTICLE 2 The White Earth Nation shall make no laws that deny the right of the people to peaceably gather or assemble for any reason, and shall make no laws that prohibit the right to petition the government for restitution, amendments, or redress of grievances, and no person shall be discriminated against for initiating or espousing an untimely or contrary petition about governance.

ARTICLE 3 The people shall not be denied the fundamental human rights of citizenship in the White Earth Nation.

ARTICLE 4 The people are equal under the law and no law, government policy, or agency practice shall discriminate in political, economic, social or cultural associations because of race, creed, sex, gender, disability, or social status.

ARTICLE 5 The freedom of thought and conscience, academic, artistic irony, and literary expression, shall not be denied, violated or controverted by the government.

ARTICLE 6 The secrecy of personal communication shall not be violated, and no censorship shall be practiced or maintained by the government.

ARTICLE 7 The right to own and transfer of private property is inviolable. The rights of property shall be protected, and private property expropriated for public use shall be according to due process of law and just compensation.

ARTICLE 8 No person shall be denied or deprived of life or liberty, except certain serious misdemeanors and felony convictions, and no criminal penalties shall be imposed without due process of law and judicial procedures.

ARTICLE 9 No person shall be apprehended by law enforcement officers without probable cause and due process of law or by warrant duly issued by a court.

ARTICLE 10 The people shall have the right to possess firearms except for convicted felons in accordance with state and federal laws.

ARTICLE 11 The people shall be secure in their homes, personal papers, and documents, against entries and electronic and material searches, without a specific, descriptive warrant for adequate cause issued by a court. Each search and seizure shall require a separate, specific warrant issued by a court, except in cases of probable threats or potential emergencies.

ARTICLE 12 No person shall be obligated to testify or provide evidence in a court against himself or herself, and any confessions obtained under compulsion, torture, or threats, or after arrest and excessive detention, may not be admissible as evidence in court. No person shall be convicted or punished for a crime when the only evidence against him or her is a confession, except in cases of crimes that can be proven by other evidence.

ARTICLE 13 No person shall be subject to trial twice for the same criminal indictment or offense.

ARTICLE 14 No person shall be denied the right to be duly informed of the nature and cause of a warrant, indictment, or criminal proceeding, and shall not be denied the right to be represented by legal counsel.

ARTICLE 15 The people shall have the right to confront and challenge witnesses in a criminal court, and the legal option of a speedy court hearing or public jury trial shall not be refused or contradicted.

ARTICLE 16 Citizens shall never be banished from the White Earth Nation.

ARTICLE 17 The Constitution of the White Earth Nation is inspired by inherent and traditional sovereignty, and contains, embodies, and promotes the rights and provisions provided in the articles and amendments of the Indian Civil Rights Act of 1968, and the United States Constitution.

Chapter 4: Sovereign Immunity

The White Earth Nation declares sovereign territorial, political, and cultural rights and powers as an independent government and immunity to civil law suits. The Legislative Council by certain formal policies and procedures shall have the right to waive the sovereign immunity of the government in the best interests of the White Earth Nation.

Chapter 5: Board of Elections

ARTICLE 1 Citizens must be at least eighteen years old to vote in government referenda and elections.

ARTICLE 2 Election and voting procedures shall be established by an Election Code and managed by an independent Board of Elections appointed by the Legislative Council.

ARTICLE 3 The Board of Elections shall consist of five eligible citizen voters of the White Earth Nation. The Chief Judge of the Board of Elections shall administer and supervise election regulations and procedures according to provisions of the Election Code. The Chief Judge shall not vote as a member of the Board of Elections.

ARTICLE 4 Members of the Board of Elections shall ensure fair and impartial elections according to the Election Code and the Constitution of the White Earth Nation.

ARTICLE 5 The Legislative Council shall resolve any challenges or allegations of impropriety of election laws or procedures.

ARTICLE 6 Citizens who become candidates for elected positions in the government shall not be members of the Board of Elections. The Legislative Council shall appoint the Chief Judge and replacements to the Board of Elections.

Chapter 6: Governance

ARTICLE 1 The White Earth Nation shall be governed by a representative and elected Legislative Council.

ARTICLE 2 The Legislative Council shall consist of a President, or White Earth Chief, the Secretary Treasurer, and elected Representatives of acknowledged communities of the White Earth Nation.

ARTICLE 3 The respective communities shall be entitled to one elected Representative to serve on the Legislative Council.

ARTICLE 4 Communities shall be established or changed by petition, by population, historic or totemic associations, and ratified by a simple majority of eligible citizen voters in a general referendum.

ARTICLE 5 The President and the Secretary Treasurer shall be elected at large by eligible citizen voters of the White Earth Nation.

Article 6 The President, Secretary Treasurer, and Representatives of the Legislative Council shall be elected for no more than two four year terms, and staggered elections shall be ordered every two years.

Article 7 Two citizens of the White Earth Nation shall be elected at large to serve constituencies outside the White Earth Reservation in the State of Minnesota.

Article 8 The Legislative Council shall have the authority to propose changes in the count of elected Representatives based on changes in population or the number of acknowledged communities. Proposals to change the count of Representatives shall be subject to a majority vote of citizens in a referendum.

Article 9 Candidates for elected government offices shall be citizens who reside within the treaty boundaries according to the Treaty of March 19, 1867, of the White Earth Nation, except two citizen members of the Legislative Council who shall be elected at large in the State of Minnesota.

Article 10 Citizens who have been convicted of a felony may vote in elections and referenda but shall not be eligible to hold elected offices in the White Earth Nation.

Article 11 Candidates for elected government office shall be at least twenty-five years of age at the time of the election.

Article 12 The Legislative Council shall appoint a new President in the event of the death, resignation, incapacity, or removal of the duly elected President. The appointed President shall serve the remainder of the elected term of the office.

Article 13 The Legislative Council has the power to initiate impeachment proceedings of elected representatives of the government for specific allegations of misconduct, criminal indictments, or felony convictions. To initiate impeachment procedures requires at least a two-thirds vote of the Legislative Council.

Article 14 There shall be two distinct procedures of impeachment. The first is admonition of misconduct but no other action or decree, and the second procedure is impeachment and removal from elected office.

ARTICLE 15 The White Earth Nation shall obligate candidates for elected offices not to disburse in campaign services, promotion and advertising more than three times the amount of the annual national family poverty guidelines for one person in the Contiguous States, established and published in the Federal Register by the United States Department of Human Services.

ARTICLE 16 Candidates for elected office shall file a formal report no later than thirty days after the election with the Chief Judge of the Board of Elections. The report shall be an affirmation of total election contributions and disbursements of the candidate.

ARTICLE 17 The President and Legislative Council of the White Earth Nation shall maintain public records and documents for posterity. The President shall nominate an archive to secure the public records and documents.

Chapter 7: Community Councils

The Community Councils shall be initiated and established in geographically based communities by citizens of the White Earth Nation. The Community Councils shall provide communal information, guidance, and recommendations to both the Legislative Council and the President on matters of concern to the citizens. The Community Councils shall promote, advance and strengthen the philosophy of mino-bimaadiziwin, to live a good life, and in good health, through the creation and formation of associations, events and activities that demonstrate, teach and encourage respect, love, bravery, humility, wisdom, honesty and truth for citizens.

Chapter 8: Council of Elders

The Council of Elders shall be nominated by citizens and designated by the Legislative Council. The Council of Elders shall provide ideas and thoughts on totemic associations, traditional knowledge, cultural and spiritual practices, native survivance, and considerations of resource management, and advise the Legislative Council. The Council of Elders shall consist of twenty citizens of the White Earth Nation who are at least fifty-five years of age at the time of appointment.

Chapter 9: Youth Council

The Youth Council shall be nominated by citizens and designated by the Legislative Council. The Youth Council shall provide information about matters that affect young people and advise the President and Legislative Council. The Youth Council shall consist of twenty citizens who are between the ages of twelve and eighteen and who are residents of the White Earth Nation.

Chapter 10: Separation of Powers

The White Earth Nation shall be divided into three separate branches of government. The Executive branch is the elected President, the Board of Elections, Council of Elders, Youth Council, and other executive designations. The Legislative branch includes the Representatives elected to the Legislative Council. The Judicial branch of government is the Judiciary and White Earth Courts. The three respective branches of government shall have no authority over any other branch, except for certain nominations and other provisions specified in the Constitution of the White Earth Nation.

Chapter 11: The President

ARTICLE 1 The President, or White Earth Chief, shall be the official national and international elected representative of the White Earth Nation.

ARTICLE 2 The President shall have the authority to secure and accept grants, negotiate agreements with associations, foundations, organizations, institutions, corporations, municipal, state, federal, and local governments, and other states and nations in the world with the ratification of the Legislative Council.

ARTICLE 3 The President shall be responsible for the administration and management of the government, and shall implement and execute the laws, ordinances, resolutions, and other enactments of the Legislative Council.

ARTICLE 4 The President shall approve by signature the laws, ordinances, measures, resolutions and appropriations of the Legislative Council.

ARTICLE 5 The President shall have the power to veto proposed laws, ordinances, measures, and resolutions initiated by the Legislative Council.

ARTICLE 6 The President shall return within five days vetoed or rejected proposed laws, ordinances and measures with a required statement of objection.

ARTICLE 7 The Legislative Council may overcome any veto of proposed laws, ordinances and resolutions by a two-thirds vote of the elected Representatives.

ARTICLE 8 The President shall have the authority to appoint executive branch administrators and other officials to serve the White Earth Nation.

ARTICLE 9 The President shall have the power to schedule and preside over sessions of the Legislative Council.

ARTICLE 10 The President shall not vote except in the case of a tie vote of the Legislative Council.

ARTICLE 11 The President shall deliver an annual address dedicated to the State of the White Earth Nation.

ARTICLE 12 The President shall be bonded as an elected official.

ARTICLE 13 The President may serve no more than two four year elected terms.

ARTICLE 14 The President shall promote, protect, and defend cultural and political sovereignty and the Constitution of the White Earth Nation.

ARTICLE 15 The President shall have the authority to nominate honorary ambassadors, consuls, citizens, and to initiate and establish embassies of the White Earth Nation to serve the national and international concerns of native survivance and moral equity.

Chapter 12: The Legislative Council

ARTICLE 1 Representatives of the Legislative Council shall propose and enact laws, codes, ordinances, resolutions, and statutes of the White Earth Nation.

ARTICLE 2 The Legislative Council shall have the authority to raise general revenue, levy and collect taxes for government services and operations, establish license and service fees, and initiate other specific levies and taxes for the welfare of the citizens of the White Earth Nation.

ARTICLE 3 The Legislative Council shall have the authority to borrow money, issue public bonds, appropriate funds for the operation of the government, and to initiate other monetary policies in the interests of the White Earth Nation.

ARTICLE 4 The Legislative Council shall promote and protect the health, public welfare, safety, education, and the cultural and political sovereignty of the citizens of the White Earth Nation.

ARTICLE 5 The Legislative Council shall establish subordinate and secondary boards, appoint delegates, and reserves the right to review the initiatives and actions of the delegates and boards.

ARTICLE 6 The Legislative Council shall be responsible for the proper management of government programs, land, waterways, resources, commerce, public housing, transportation, casino operations, business enterprises, and other assets of the White Earth Nation.

ARTICLE 7 The Legislative Council shall have the authority to control the distribution and sale of alcoholic beverages within the treaty boundaries of the White Earth Nation.

ARTICLE 8 The Legislative Council shall not establish, support, or embody any covert political, military, or intelligence operations, without due process of law and legal warrants, against peaceable citizens of the White Earth Nation.

Article 9 The Legislative Council shall have residual powers, and the powers of governance provided, specified, and entrusted in the Constitution shall not be construed as the limitation of legislative power or authority. The powers of the government not specifically expressed or entrusted to the Legislative Council shall be reserved to the citizens of the White Earth Nation.

Chapter 13: The Secretary Treasurer

Article 1 The Secretary Treasurer shall be bonded and responsible for monetary and financial matters, resources, documents and records of the Legislative Council. Government records shall be available for public inspection and review.

Article 2 The Secretary Treasurer shall schedule an annual audit of funds, monetary transactions and records, deposits, and expenditures by a duly certified independent auditor.

Article 3 The Secretary Treasurer shall carry through official duties and responsibilities of the President and the Representatives of the Legislative Council.

Article 4 The Secretary Treasurer shall be a voting member of the Legislative Council.

Article 5 The Secretary Treasure shall provide and publish an annual fiscal report and accounting of the White Earth Nation.

Chapter 14: The Judiciary

Article 1 The Judiciary shall consist of the White Earth Court, Court of Appeals, and other courts established by the Legislative Council.

Article 2 The White Earth Court shall have the power of judicial review and jurisdiction over any legal matters, disputes, civil procedures and criminal laws, ordinances, regulations, codes and customs of family relations, protection, and dissolution, adoption, domestic violence, juvenile justice, and probate, housing and property, conservation, taxation, governance, the corporate code, election disputes, and constitutional issues of the White Earth Nation.

ARTICLE 3 The Court of Appeals shall have original and appellate jurisdiction. The Court of Appeals shall hear case appeals and issues initiated by the Legislative Council. Decisions of the Court of Appeals are conclusive.

Chapter 15: Powers of the White Earth Courts

ARTICLE 1 The Courts shall have the authority to interpret and construe the laws, ordinances, and regulations of the Legislative Council and the Constitution of the White Earth Nation.

ARTICLE 2 The Courts shall issue legal decisions, injunctions, reviews, writs of mandamus, extradition, certiorari, writs of habeas corpus, and other legal orders, instruments, and documents.

ARTICLE 3 The Courts shall establish procedures, rules, legal forms, and review by formal requests of citizens the specific and comprehensive constitutional validity of laws, ordinances, and codes initiated and passed by the Legislative Council.

ARTICLE 4 The Courts shall ensure and practice restorative justice in civil actions, minor criminal offenses, juvenile and family matters, whenever appropriate to resolve complaints and disputes of the White Earth Nation.

ARTICLE 5 The Courts shall establish and publish a code of judicial ethics.

Chapter 16: The White Earth Judges

ARTICLE 1 The White Earth Court shall consist of a Chief Judge and Associate Judges. The Chief Judge shall be appointed and removed by the Legislative Council.

ARTICLE 2 The Chief Judge shall appoint the necessary number of Associate Judges for five-year terms with the consent of the Legislative Council.

ARTICLE 3 The Court of Appeals shall consist of three judges and shall be appointed by the Legislative Council in consultation with the Chief Judge.

ARTICLE 4 The Chief Judge shall not be a member of the Court of Appeals.

ARTICLE 5 Judges of the Court of Appeals shall serve for five years, and may otherwise practice law or be associated with a law firm.

ARTICLE 6 The judges of the courts shall be at least twenty-five years of age, of proven moral character, and have not been convicted of a felony.

ARTICLE 7 The judges shall be graduates of a law school accredited by the American Bar Association.

ARTICLE 8 The judges shall be admitted to the bar to practice law in native communities, state, or federal courts.

ARTICLE 9 The judges shall be experienced lawyers, magistrates, or judges.

ARTICLE 10 The judges shall have knowledge of Anishinaabe culture, traditions, and general history.

ARTICLE 11 The judges shall recuse themselves, an assertion of judicial disqualification, as unsuitable to perform legal duties where there are possible conflicts of interest, or the appearance of personal interests, or potential challenges of partiality.

ARTICLE 12 The judges shall be impeached by the Legislative Council and removed from judicial practice for abuses of impartiality, bribery, political impropriety, or felony conviction.

Chapter 17: Legislative Council Meetings

ARTICLE 1 The Legislative Council shall meet at least once each month to conduct government business. The time and place of each session shall be posted in advance.

ARTICLE 2 Citizens of the White Earth Nation have the right to attend sessions of the Legislative Council.

ARTICLE 3 The President has the authority to schedule special and emergency sessions of the Legislative Council.

ARTICLE 4 The Legislative Council by a majority vote and written request shall have the authority to schedule a special session.

ARTICLE 5 The President shall be obligated to schedule a special session of the Legislative Council by an official petition of thirty percent of eligible citizen voters of the White Earth Nation.

ARTICLE 6 The President may schedule an emergency session of the Legislative Council without written notice to consider urgent matters, services, protection of the health, welfare and safety of the citizens and communities of the White Earth Nation.

ARTICLE 7 The Legislative Council shall conduct no other business than the specific stated purpose of an emergency session.

ARTICLE 8 The Legislative Council shall have the authority to meet in closed executive sessions with the President to discuss matters of litigation, proposed and discreet negotiations, and other concerns of confidentiality.

ARTICLE 9 The Legislative Council shall not decide actions on matters of litigation or confidentiality in closed executive sessions except when the outcome of the session has been fully reported in subsequent public sessions of the Legislative Council. The results of executive sessions shall be decided by vote at a public meeting.

ARTICLE 10 Legislative Council motions, votes, resolutions and decisions shall be noted and preserved in the official minutes of the sessions.

ARTICLE 11 Legislative Council actions, decisions, and enactments of record shall be available for inspection by citizens during normal business hours of the government.

ARTICLE 12 The Legislative Council shall date and number each and every resolution, ordinance, law and statute, and cite the appropriate authority of the Constitution of the White Earth Nation.

ARTICLE 13 The Legislative Council shall prepare a certificate for each resolution, ordinance, and statute that confirms the presence of a quorum and indicates the number of members voting for or against each enactment.

ARTICLE 14 The Legislative Council shall constitute a quorum by a simple majority of fifty-one percent of the elected members at a duly scheduled session.

Chapter 18: Ethics and Impeachment

ARTICLE 1 Elected members of the government may be impeached or removed from office by a recorded two-thirds vote of the entire Legislative Council.

ARTICLE 2 The Legislative Council may impeach or remove from office an elected member of government for a felony conviction in a court of competent jurisdiction.

ARTICLE 3 The Legislative Council may impeach or remove from office an elected member of the government for two misdemeanor convictions, including driving while intoxicated, but not including ordinary traffic violations.

ARTICLE 4 Elected officials of the government may not be suspended or removed from office without due process of law.

ARTICLE 5 The Legislative Council may impeach for cause an elected member of the government. The impeachment may be a form of admonition, a warning or legal statement of charges, or the impeachment may be based on an indictment or conviction for a felony, and the forcible removal of an official of the government.

ARTICLE 6 The White Earth Nation shall provide for a recall election of an elected official of the government. Citizens have the right to initiate a petition to recall an elected official. The petition shall secure at least two-thirds of the eligible voters for a recall election. The petition may be political and may include allegations, grievances, complaints and assertions of misconduct, nonfeasance, or mismanagement by an elected official of the government.

Chapter 19: Petitions and Referenda

ARTICLE 1 The Legislative Council may initiate a referendum by a vote of two-thirds of the elected Representatives.

ARTICLE 2 Citizens of the White Earth Nation may initiate a referendum by evidence of a vote of thirty percent of the eligible citizen voters.

ARTICLE 3 The Legislative Council and eligible citizens may present proposed laws, ordinances, and initiatives to a referendum vote of the electorate, according to certified evidence of the constitutional process.

ARTICLE 4 The referendum vote shall be held within one hundred and eighty days from the official receipt of the petition, unless the scheduled date of the referendum is within six months of a general election, in which event the referendum would be presented to the eligible voters in the general election.

ARTICLE 5 Scheduled referenda shall be conducted according to the rules and regulations of the Board of Elections and the Election Code.

Chapter 20: Amendments to the Constitution

The Constitution of the White Earth Nation may be amended by two-thirds of the recorded eligible votes in a duly called election or referendum to amend the Constitution. Eligible voters must be formally informed by written and published notices of the proposed amendment to the Constitution of the White Earth Nation.

Ratification of the Constitution

The sworn delegates to the White Earth Constitutional Convention hereby duly ratify for a citizen referendum the Constitution of the White Earth Nation.

The Constitution of the White Earth Nation was duly ratified on April 4, 2009, at the Shooting Star Casino Hotel, Mahnomen, Minnesota.

The ratification was by secret ballots of twenty-four delegates present. Sixteen delegates voted for ratification, and eight delegates voted against ratification.

Gerald Vizenor, distinguished professor of American Studies at the University of New Mexico, was a delegate to the Constitutional Convention and the principal writer of the proposed Constitution of the White Earth Nation.

The Constitution Proposal Team included Erma Vizenor, president of the White Earth Nation; Jill May Doerfler, assistant professor, Department of Indian Studies, University of Minnesota, Duluth; Jo Anne E. Stately, vice president of development for the Indian Land Tenure Foundation; and Anita Fineday, chief tribal court judge, White Earth Nation. David E. Wilkins, professor of American Indian Studies, University of Minnesota, was a special consultant to the Constitutional Convention and the proposal team.

Jill Doerfler

A Citizen's Guide to the White Earth Constitution

HIGHLIGHTS AND REFLECTIONS

These eight essays were first published in *Anishinaabeg Today: A Chronicle of the White Earth Band of Ojibwe,* the official newspaper of the White Earth Nation. The articles were written with the intention of sharing information with the Anishinaabeg citizens of White Earth Reservation in preparation for a referendum vote on the ratified Constitution of the White Earth Nation. Source information appears at the end of each article.

Rebuilding and Renewing Tribal Sovereignty

White Earth is one of many American Indian nations currently engaging in the process of constitutional reform, reclaiming the right to govern themselves, and creating a future full of promise. Many American Indian nations wrote constitutions in the 1930s after the passage of the Indian Reorganization Act (IRA) of 1934 and were highly influenced and, in some cases, pressured by U.S. officials. As Vine Deloria Jr. and Clifford M. Lytle argue in *The Nations Within: The Past and Future of American Indian Sovereignty,* "it is crucial to realize . . . that these have not been the forms of government that the Indian people themselves have demanded or appreciated and are certainly not the kind of government that most Indians, given a truly free choice in the matter, would have adopted by themselves." Today tribes are working to remove the colonial legacies imposed in IRA constitutions and are embracing the opportunity to remake constitutions into documents that reflect the culture, values, and beliefs of their citizens. The Minnesota Chippewa Tribe (MCT) was created under the Indian Reorganization Act; the preamble of that Constitution even states that "tribal organization" were created "in accordance with such privilege granted the Indians by the United States under existing law." This kind of language undermines tribal sovereignty, but is common in IRA constitutions. Tribal sovereignty is inherent and is not a privilege that the United States has granted Native nations. The MCT constitution also gives a significant amount of power to the U.S. secretary of the interior. The ratified White Earth Constitution does not delineate any power to the United States.

As Anishinaabe scholar Duane Champagne argues in *Remaking Tribal Constitutions,* if "tribal communities want to assert greater control over their economic, political, and cultural lives, they will need more effective forms of government. For many communities there is a growing sense of crisis and a movement to remake tribal constitutions." The time has come for tribal nations to rebuild. As part of that process, many tribal nations are working to create constitutions that incorporate their values and traditions. Blood quantum was imposed upon many tribes by the BIA and federal officials. The Minnesota Chippewa Tribe did not begin to use the one-quarter MCT blood requirement for tribal citizenship until it was pressured into doing so in the 1960s. Other tribal nations had similar experiences. For example, the Fort Peck Tribe in Montana used lineal descent before it accepted a blood quantum requirement along with other constitutional changes in 1960. According to the current

Fort Peck Tribes Constitution, enrolled members must be at least one-quarter Assiniboine or Sioux, or a combination of the two. This requirement has divided families. Roberta Garfield, a Fort Peck citizen and grandmother of twenty-four children, has commented, "We have to claim our grandkids." Garfield supports lineal descent. Efforts toward constitutional reform are ongoing at Fort Peck. (The quotations in this paragraph come from Andrea Appleton's article, "Blood Quantum: A Complicated System that Determines Tribal Membership Threatens the Future of American Indians," published in *High Country News* on January 19, 2009.)

Declining enrollments and cultural revitalization have influenced many tribes to consider constitutional changes and to consider how best to define citizenship criteria. Legal scholar Scott L. Gould has observed in "Mixing Bodies and Beliefs: The Predicament of Tribes" that many of these tribes will have to decide "whether to continue emphasizing race as the central criterion for membership, or to search for other measures of affinity." As the racial diversity of American Indians continues to increase, questions abound as to how a viable citizenship base can be maintained using racial standards such as one-quarter blood quantum. American Indians are the most racially diverse group in the United States, and they have the highest rates of intermarriage. Gould also states: "Cultural survival for most tribes may depend on eliminating race as the essential criterion for membership." It is not only culture that is at stake; it is American Indian nations themselves. Based on current citizenship requirements, many tribes will have no new citizens in fifty years and even more will face the same fate in a century. Blood quantum is mathematical termination. Once Native nations "disappear," the U.S. government will finally be free of their treaty and fiscal responsibilities. In an effort to prevent this situation, many tribes are changing citizenship requirements to ensure that their nations will continue in perpetuity.

Cultural revitalization is another motivation for the creation of new citizenship requirements. Many tribes want to find practical ways to incorporate values and traditions. Citizenship offers an opportunity to enact cultural practices. The ratified Constitution of the White Earth Nation uses lineal descent as the basis for citizenship. This prioritizes family relationships and ensures that the nation will never "disappear" due to a lack of citizens. Eliminating the one-quarter blood quantum requirement is also part of the decolonization process and a demonstration of sovereignty. One of the most fundamental powers any nation has is to decide citizenship requirements. When the U.S. secretary of the interior rejected MCT resolutions requiring lineal descent for tribal citizenship, it was an infringement upon tribal sovereignty. Now White Earth has a historic opportunity to take back citizenship requirements. This is a chance to rebuild and renew our sovereignty.

Anishinaabeg Today 15, no. 8 (August 4, 2010): 9, 17.

Families First: Tribal Citizenship and the White Earth Nation

The constitutional delegates spent a significant amount of time discussing a number of different options for citizenship. Each of the options discussed had its pros and cons. There is no doubt that tribal citizenship is an emotional and personal issue with no easy answer. The delegates worked through the issue and came up with a solution that honors the wishes of our ancestors and ensures a vibrant future for the seventh generation. The regulation of tribal citizenship puts our values into action; citizenship regulation is a way of practicing and living our culture.

Citizenship carries both rights and responsibilities. Active citizenship focuses on how we can be productive citizens who contribute to the nation, not on what we can get from our White Earth government. A citizen has several responsibilities and duties: some of the most familiar include obeying the laws enacted by one's government and participating to improve the quality of political and civic life.

Some delegates rejected the use of blood quantum for tribal citizenship for a number of reasons. The federal government began the practice of using blood quantum to define American Indians as a calculated way of eliminating numerous people who would otherwise be legally identified as American Indian. Blood quantum is a premeditated form of termination. Blood quantum racializes American Indian identity and takes the focus off political status. Blood quantum presumes that all aspects of your national ancestry can be divided out and total 100 percent. An individual might be 17 percent German, 32 percent French, 25 percent Minnesota Chippewa, and so on. It is generally assumed that the fractions mirror cultural practices, knowledge, and loyalties. However this is not the case—a person who is one-half Anishinaabe does not necessarily participate in more cultural activities nor have a stronger connection to community than a person who is one-quarter Anishinaabe. Another example would be that an individual with three-quarters Anishinaabe "blood" does not automatically know how to speak three-quarters of the language: again, this is a cultural practice that one would learn either as a child in the home or by taking language classes as an adult. These things are not biological, but instead are generally determined by how a person was raised; they are not exact reflections of blood quantum. Thus, many people believe that being Anishinaabe is about much more than just biology or race—it is about culture and the way we live our lives, which is not something that can be divided into fractions. If blood quantum does not directly reflect our cultural practices, beliefs or political loyalties, we must consider why we continue to use it as the sole determiner of tribal citizenship.

The delegates decided that citizenship should reflect our values and beliefs. At the heart of this issue is the question: "What makes an individual Anishinaabe?" or, more specifically, "What makes an individual a citizen of the White Earth Nation?" There is no easy answer to this question. For most people being Anishinaabe is a combination of lineage, culture, and political status.

A majority of the delegates agreed that lineal descent is the best way to honor our ancestors and ensure a vibrant future for the seventh generation. Lineal descent will ensure that there will always be a White Earth Nation. It allows for growth and change but keeps the fundamental familial relationship as the base. Lineal descent puts our families first. The constitutional delegates have completed their work; ultimately, it will be up to White Earth citizens to decide whether they approve the ratified Constitution in a referendum vote. White Earth citizens must ask themselves whether they want to continue to follow the wishes of the United States and perpetuate a nation based on pseudo-scientific measurements of "blood" or move forward and put our families first.

Anishinaabeg Today 14, no. 9 (August 5, 2009): 2, 23.

Restoring Power to the People

The Indian Reorganization Act (IRA) constitutions have received considerable criticism because they generally do not reflect the specific cultural values and practices of the Native nations. One thing many citizens, leaders, and scholars have pointed out is that most IRA constitutions do not have a bill of rights to protect citizens. In fact, the Constitution of the Minnesota Chippewa Tribe has a very few specific protections for the rights of citizens buried in article 13, "Rights of Members." Many people find it is essential to have a bill of rights to prevent abuses of power; a bill of rights represents the power held by the people. A government has a responsibility to clearly define the rights of citizens so those rights can be protected, violations identified, and corrections made. The people (citizens) are the nation's source of power; a nation must have citizens or it will cease to exist.

The seventeen articles in the constitutional chapter "Rights and Duties" describe important civil liberties and human rights guaranteed to the citizens of the White Earth Nation. This chapter is entitled "Rights and Duties" because both the government and the citizens have duties (or responsibilities) and rights. Some of the articles protect freedom of thought and expression, and the government may not practice censorship. Several articles ensure due process of law and protect privacy against search and seizure by requiring a warrant. Article 16 prohibits the practice of banishment.

Anishinaabeg Today 15, no. 9 (September 1, 2010): 8, 11.

Governance of the White Earth Nation

The constitutional chapter entitled "Governance" sets out the basic terms and creates a representative and elected governing body: the Legislative Council. Each community will have one representative on the Legislative Council; article 4 explains how communities will be established. There is not a fixed number of representatives, nor are there fixed borders, nor is there a constitutional definition of what constitutes a community: the people will decide these details in a referendum vote. Not providing this detail in the Constitution allows for change and adaptation to population shifts over time. There are many White Earth citizens who live outside the boundaries set forth in the Treaty of March 19, 1867, but who still live within the boundaries of the state of Minnesota. The chapter provides for two Legislative Council representatives to represent these individuals. The president and secretary treasurer will be elected at large, as they are now.

There are several other important features in this chapter. First of all, a term limit of two terms (eight years) in any single position is established in article 6. There are currently no term limits, although many delegates supported the creation of term limits because such limits ensure new leadership. As stated in article 10, citizens who have been convicted of a felony may vote but cannot hold elected office. As a means to hold leaders accountable, articles 13 and 14 clearly lay out two distinct processes for impeachment. Article 15 establishes campaign spending limits; this is revolutionary for a tribal constitution. I know of no other Native nation with campaign spending limits; many scholars have speculated that a lack of campaign finance laws leaves Native nations vulnerable. Spending limits also makes running for office accessible to a wide portion of the population.

Anishinaabeg Today 15, no. 10 (October 6, 2010): 6.

Delegates Want More Ways to Engage Leaders

The constitutional chapters "Community Councils," "Council of Elders," and "Youth Council" are closely related. Each chapter creates and formally recognizes councils and establishes the various roles that each council has. White Earth does already have some similar councils in place now that do a wonderful job. Including these councils in the Constitution is important because it gives formal recognition to the councils and gives them increased authority. During the convention process, many constitutional delegates discussed the desire for more ways to engage with and advise elected leaders. It was important to find ways to have multiple voices heard and it was decided that Community Councils, a Council of Elders, and a Youth Council would be a good way to include a broad range of input. These formal councils are one way citizens can organize and make recommendations to both members of the Legislative Council and the president.

Historically, advisory councils were very important in many systems of Native governance. Advisory councils shared their perspectives with leaders and also held them accountable for their decisions. Leaders wanted advice and guidance from the people because it helped them make the best possible decisions. Leaders would also come to the councils with questions. Constitutional delegates wanted to restore and create lines of communication between elected leaders and the three advisory councils established in the Constitution. In addition, the councils provide opportunities for citizens to speak with and listen to the ideas and perspectives of other citizens. Councils can work together to come to consensus on what is best for all. The seven teachings were incorporated into the "Community Councils" chapter. Geographically based communities would utilize or establish Community Councils, just as they do now. The Council of Elders and the Youth Council will be at large bodies. The Constitution provides a basic framework and these councils would create their own specific bylaws or other governing documents.

Anishinaabeg Today 15, no. 11 (November 3, 2010): 5.

The White Earth Constitution Balances Power

The constitutional chapters "Separation of Powers" and "The President" create a balance of power between different branches of the governance structure. One consistent critique of IRA constitutions is the lack of separation of powers. Indeed, the MCT Constitution does not have a separation of powers. Many countries around the world have a system of governance that includes some form of separation of powers. Historically, American Indian nations also distributed power to different groups of people, which functioned much as separation of powers does today. Constitutional delegates agreed that the White Earth Constitution should separate powers into different branches of government. The branches of government in the White Earth Constitution are the executive, the legislative, and the judicial. A separation of powers balances power between different branches of government. Each branch has powers that it can exercise to balance the other branches. For example, under the White Earth Constitution the president can veto legislation passed by the Legislative Council; however, the Legislative Council can override a veto with a two-thirds majority. In this system, the power of both the president and the Legislative Council are balanced in a reasonable manner so that neither has supreme authority.

The chapter "The President" also contains many significant changes from the current governance structure. It outlines the powers of the president, who is the head of the government. The authority of the president is balanced by the Legislative Council and the judiciary. For example, the president has the authority to negotiate agreements with other governments but the agreements will not be final and binding until ratified by the Legislative Council. The president does not have the authority to create laws, ordinances, or resolutions but does have the responsibility to execute them. Another important change is the institution of term limits. The president may only be elected to two four-year terms. Term limits ensure leadership turnover and limit the ability of individuals to become career politicians.

Anishinaabeg Today 15, no. 12 (December 1, 2010): 8, 12.

Delegates Expressed Desire for More Representatives

The constitutional chapters "The Legislative Council" and "The Secretary Treasurer" outline the primary duties, rights, and responsibilities of the representatives elected to the Legislative Council and of the secretary treasurer. As stated in the constitutional chapter "Governance," all elected representatives are subject to a maximum of two four-year terms. The Legislative Council forms the primary governing body of the White Earth Nation. During the reform process, many constitutional delegates expressed a desire for a larger number of representatives. The number of representatives elected to the Legislative Council will be determined by a referendum vote. It is likely that the number of representatives on the Legislative Council will change over time as the population changes; however, any changes must be approved by a referendum vote.

The Legislative Council has several important duties and responsibilities. One of the primary duties is to propose and enact laws, codes, ordinances, resolutions, and statutes. Any legislation passed by the Legislative Council must be approved by the president; if it is vetoed, the Legislative Council must have a two-thirds majority to override the veto. The Legislative Council has many duties relating to the management of government programs and the business dealings of the White Earth nation. The Legislative Council also has the responsibility to "promote and protect the health, public welfare, safety, education, and the cultural and political sovereignty of the citizens of the White Earth Nation."

Many of the duties of the secretary treasurer will remain the same as they are now. The primary duties are all related to the financial matters of the White Earth Nation. The secretary treasurer is required to make certain financial documents available for public viewing. This requirement ensures an open process and allows White Earth citizens to hold elected leaders accountable for the financial dealings of the nation.

Anishinaabeg Today 16, no. 1 (January 5, 2011): 6, 18.

White Earth Constitution: Judicial System

The constitutional chapters "The Judiciary," "Powers of the White Earth Courts," and "The White Earth Judges" establish a judiciary and its foundational powers. Many constitutional delegates felt it was important to have the judicial system in the Constitution because it provides a strong foundation and clearly states how the courts and judges do and don't engage with the other parts of the government. They also wanted a system of courts as opposed to a single court. The Constitution establishes the White Earth Court and Court of Appeals but also allows the

Legislative Council to establish other courts. While White Earth currently has a court system (see www.whiteearthtribalcourt.com), this system was created outside the Constitution.

The judiciary cannot make laws, but the court may invalidate laws that conflict with the Constitution. The judiciary does not enforce laws. The main role of the judiciary is to interpret and apply laws, statues, ordinances, and other regulations. Another role of the judiciary is to resolve disputes. Constitutional delegates emphasized a desire to utilize restorative justice, and this is reflected in article 4 of "Powers of the White Earth Courts." Like Anishinaabe traditional values, restorative justice places an emphasis on healing and restoring balance for all parties involved. Restorative justice places a focus on relationships and encourages communication between victims and offenders. Offenders must take responsibility for their actions.

As listed in the chapter, judges must meet many requirements. A judge must be at least twenty-five years old, be a graduate of a law school accredited by the American Bar Association, and have knowledge of Anishinaabe culture, traditions, and general history. The Legislative Council will appoint the chief judge. Associate judges will have five-year terms and be appointed by the chief judge, with the consent of the Legislative Council. The Legislative Council has the authority to impeach and remove judges for abuses of impartiality, bribery, political impropriety, or felony conviction.

Anishinaabeg Today 16, no. 2 (February 2, 2011): 4.

White Earth Constitution: Accountability

The final four constitutional chapters, "Legislative Council Meetings," "Ethics and Impeachment," "Petitions and Referenda," and "Amendments to the Constitution," deal with a variety of important technical procedures related to accountability.

The constitutional chapter "Legislative Council Meetings"

describes procedural issues relating to meetings of the Legislative Council. The level of detail provides assurances to citizens that (with the noted emergency exceptions) meetings will be both publicly announced and open. Additionally, Legislative Council motions, votes, resolutions, and decisions must be recorded in the official minutes of the sessions. The decisions made by the Legislative Council must be available for examination by citizens. These provisions ensure transparency and permit citizens to be informed of all actions taken by the government. This important information allows citizens to know exactly what the actions of their representatives are and will impact reelection.

The constitutional chapter "Ethics and Impeachment" provides ways to hold elected leaders to ethical standards and, if those standards are not met, to impeach them. Citizens do their best to elect good leaders. There are times when it becomes necessary to remove a leader from office. Many constitutional delegates expressed a desire to hold elected officials to high standards and to ensure that elected officials could be removed from office should it become necessary. Article 1 provides for impeachment and removal from office with a two-thirds majority vote by the Legislative Council. An elected official may be impeached or removed from office for a felony conviction or for two misdemeanor convictions, including driving while intoxicated but not including ordinary traffic violations. Holding leaders to these high ethical standards is based on our traditional values. In addition, article 6 ensures that citizens can initiate a petition to recall an elected official. At least two-thirds of eligible voters must sign a petition to initiate a recall election. There are a variety of reasons for a petition, including allegations of misconduct or mismanagement by an elected official.

The constitutional chapter "Petitions and Referenda" explains the process for petitions and referendum votes. A referendum is a form of direct democracy in which citizens have a direct voice. Referenda can be binding or non-binding. Non-binding referenda are advisory and could be used to help the Legislative Council or the president to make decisions. The Legislative Council and, by petition, the citizens retain the power to initiate a referendum. While members of the Legislative Council will make many important decisions for the people, there are also times when the Legislative Council may determine that a referendum vote is the best way to address an issue. The Legislative Council must have a two-thirds majority vote to hold a referendum. Article 3 establishes that citizens can present petitions requesting a referendum vote. If a petition passes the certification process, a vote must be held within 180 days from the official receipt of the petition. The only exception is if the scheduled date of the referendum is within six months of a general election, in which case the referendum would be presented to the eligible voters in the general election. There are two primary reasons for the exception to the 180-day rule: first, holding a referendum close to a general election could have negative or unforeseen consequences during the general election; secondly, holding a referendum election is expensive, so this is also related to fiscal responsibility. When referenda can be combined with a general election, cost savings are significant.

The final constitutional chapter, "Amendments to the Constitution," specifies the procedures for constitutional amendments. A constitution is a living document. The ability to amend the Constitution is critical so that it can adapt to the changing needs and will of the people. Neither the Legislative Council nor the president has the authority to amend the Constitution; only the people have the power to amend the Constitution through a referendum vote.

Anishinaabeg Today 16, no. 3 (March 2, 2011): 4, 13.

Bibliography

Appleton, Andrea. "Blood Quantum: A Complicated System that Determines Tribal Membership Threatens the Future of American Indians." *High Country News* (January 19, 2009). http://www.hcn .org/issues/41.1/blood-quantum.

Ashley, Mike. *Taking Liberties: The Struggle for Britain's Freedoms and Rights.* London: British Library, 2008.

Bailyn, Bernard. *To Begin the World Anew.* New York: Alfred A. Knopf, 2003.

——, ed. *The Debates of the Constitution, Part One.* New York: Library of America Press, 1993.

——, ed. *The Debates of the Constitution, Part Two.* New York: Library of America Press, 1993.

Barber, Benjamin. "Constitutional Rights—Democratic Instrument or Obstacle?" In *The Framers and Fundamental Rights,* edited by Robert A. Licht. Washington DC: American Enterprise Press, 1992.

Barsh, Russell. "The Nature and Spirit of North American Political Systems." *American Indian Quarterly* (Summer 1986).

Beard, Charles A. *An Economic Interpretation of the Constitution of the United States.* Mineola NY: Dover Publications, 2004. First published 1913 by Macmillan, New York.

Best, Judith. "Fundamental Rights and the Structure of the Government." In *The Framers and Fundamental Rights*, edited by Robert A. Licht. Washington DC: American Enterprise Press, 1992.

Bingham, Tom. *The Rule of Law.* London: Allen Lane, 2010.

Boyd, Brian. *On the Origin of Stories.* Cambridge MA: Belknap Press of Harvard University, 2009.

Brown, Mark H. *The Flight of the Nez Perce.* New York: Putnam, 1967.

Champagne, Duane. "Remaking Tribal Constitutions: Meeting the Challenges of Tradition, Colonialism, and Globalization." In *American Indian Constitutional Reform and the Rebuilding of Native Nations*, edited by Eric D. Lemont. Austin: University of Texas Press, 2006.

Cohen, Felix S. *On the Drafting of Tribal Constitutions.* Edited by David E. Wilkins. Norman: University of Oklahoma Press, 2006.

Colley, Linda. *Taking Stock of Taking Liberties.* London: British Library, 2008.

Connor, Walker. *Ethnonationalism: The Quest for Understanding.* Princeton NJ: Princeton University Press, 1994.

The Constitution of the White Earth Nation. Mahnomen MN: *Anishinaabeg Today*, White Earth Reservation Newspaper, May 6, 2009.

Dahl, Robert A. *How Democratic Is the American Constitution?* New Haven CT: Yale University Press, 2001.

The Declaration of Independence and the Constitution of the United States. Washington DC: Cato Institute, 1998.

Deloria, Ella. *Speaking for Indians.* Lincoln: University of Nebraska Press, 1998.

Deloria, Vine, Jr. *Custer Died for Your Sins: An Indian Manifesto.* Norman: University of Oklahoma Press, 1988.

———. *The Nations Within: The Past and Future of American Indian Sovereignty.* Austin: University of Texas Press, 1998.

Deloria, Vine, Jr., and Clifford M. Lytle. *American Indians, American Justice.* Austin: University of Texas Press, 1983.

Deutsch, Karl Wolfgang. *Nationalism and Its Alternatives.* New York: Random House, 1969.

Fritz, Christian G. *American Sovereigns: The People and America's Constitutional Tradition before the Civil War.* Cambridge UK: Cambridge University Press, 2008.

Gould, Scott L. "Mixing Bodies and Beliefs: The Predicament of Tribes." *Columbia Law Review* 101, no. 4 (May 2001).

Halfmoon, Otis. "Joseph (Heinmot Tooyalakekt)." In *Encyclopedia of North American Indians*, edited by Frederick E. Hoxie. Boston: Houghton Mifflin, 1996.

Halliday, Paul D. *Habeas Corpus: From England to Empire*. Cambridge MA: Harvard University Press, 2010.

Hampton, Bruce. *Children of Grace: The Nez Perce War of 1877*. New York: Henry Holt, 1994.

Joseph (chief), "An Indian's View of Indian Affairs." *North American Review*, April 1879.

Lemont, Eric D., ed. *American Indian Constitutional Reform*. Austin: University of Texas Press, 2006.

Levy, Leonard W. *Origins of the Bill of Rights*. New Haven CT: Yale University Press, 1999.

Lewis, Anthony. *Freedom for the Thought That We Hate*. New York: Basic Books, 2007.

Licht, Robert A., ed. *The Framers and Fundamental Rights*. Washington DC: American Enterprise Press, 1992.

Linebaugh, Peter. *The Magna Carta Manifesto*. Berkeley: University of California Press, 2008.

McGuire, Robert A. "Economic Interests and the Adoption of the United States Constitution." http://eh.net/encyclopedia/article /mcguire.constitution.us.economic.interests. Accessed February 1, 2010.

———. *To Form a More Perfect Union: A New Economic Interpretation of the United States Constitution*. New York: Oxford University Press, 2003.

Morgan, Edmund. *Inventing the People: The Rise of Popular Sovereignty in England and America*. New York: W. W. Norton, 1989.

Prucha, Francis Paul. *American Indian Treaties: The History of a Political Anomaly*. Berkeley: University of California Press, 1994.

———. *The Indians in American Society*. Berkeley: University of California Press, 1985.

———, ed. *Documents of United States Indian Policy*. Lincoln: University of Nebraska Press, 1975.

Rancière, Jacques. *Hatred of Democracy*. London: Verso, 2006.

Rosenfeld, Michel. *The Identity of the Constitutional Subject: Selfhood, Citizenship, Culture, and Community.* London: Routledge, 2010.

Tribe, Laurence H. *The Invisible Constitution.* New York: Oxford University Press, 2008.

U.S. Supreme Court Reports. Towne v. Eisner, 245 U.S. 418 (1918).

Vizenor, Gerald. *Native Liberty: Natural Reason and Cultural Survivance.* Lincoln: University of Nebraska Press, 2009.

———. *The People Named the Chippewa: Narrative Histories.* Minneapolis: University of Minnesota Press, 1984.

Waldstreicher, David. *Slavery's Constitution: From Revolution to Ratification.* New York: Hill and Wang, 2009.

Warren, William W. *History of the Ojibway Nation.* Minneapolis: Ross & Haines, 1957. First published 1885 by the Minnesota Historical Society.

Wilkins, David E. *American Indian Sovereignty and the U.S. Supreme Court.* Austin: University of Texas Press, 1997.

Wolin, Sheldon S. *The Presence of the Past: Essays on the State of the Constitution.* Baltimore: Johns Hopkins University Press, 1989.

Contributors

GERALD VIZENOR is distinguished professor of American Studies at the University of New Mexico, Albuquerque, and professor emeritus of American Studies at the University of California, Berkeley. He was a delegate to the Constitutional Convention and the principal writer of the Constitution of the White Earth Nation. Vizenor is the author of more than thirty books on Native histories, critical studies, and literature, including *The People Named the Chippewa: Narrative Histories,* and *Manifest Manners: Narratives on Postindian Survivance.* His most recent books include *Fugitive Poses: Native American Indian Scenes of Absence and Presence, Native Liberty: Natural Reason and Cultural Survivance,* a selection of essays, *Survivance: Narratives of Native Presence,* and *Native Storiers,* an anthology of contemporary Native American literature. Professor Vizenor is a series editor, with Diane Glancy, of Native Storiers at the University of Nebraska Press. He is also a series editor, with Deborah Madsen, of Native Traces at the State University of New York Press.

Jill Doerfler, assistant professor of American Indian Studies at the University of Minnesota, Duluth, coordinated and participated in the deliberations and the ratification of the Constitution of the White Earth Nation. She edited *Centering Anishinaabeg Studies: Understanding the World Through Stories* (forthcoming in 2013) with Niigonwedom James Sinclair and Heidi Kiiwetinepinesiik Stark. Professor Doerfler has also published several essays in journals, a series of articles in *Aninishinaabeg Today: A Chronicle of the White Earth Band of Ojibwe*, and is currently completing a book manuscript, *Blood v. Family: The Struggle Over Identity and Tribal Citizenship Among the White Earth Anishinaabeg*.

David E. Wilkins is professor of American Indian Studies and adjunct professor of Political Science, Law, and American Studies at the University of Minnesota. He is the author of many books, including *American Indian Sovereignty and the U.S. Supreme Court*, *American Indian Politics and the American Political System*, and, with Tsianina Lomawaima, *Uneven Ground: American Indian Sovereignty and Federal Law*.

Milton Keynes UK
Ingram Content Group UK Ltd.
UKHW040101181223
434413UK00015B/134

9 780803 240797